BODY MIND & SPIRIT

LOUIS HUGHES

BODY
MIND &
SPIRIT

TO
HARMONY
THROUGH
MEDITATION

TWENTY-THIRD PUBLICATIONS
Mystic, Connecticut

Dedicated to Kerry

Source and inspiration for this book

Illustrations by William Baker and A. Alcock.

North American Edition 1991

Twenty-Third Publications
P.O. Box 180
185 Willow Street
Mystic, CT 06355
(203) 536-2611

ISBN 0-89622-484-8
Library of Congress Catalog Card No. 91-65004

Originally published as *Body-Mind Meditation: A Gateway to Spirituality* by the Mercier Press, 4 Bridge Street, Cork and 24 Lower Abbey Street, Dublin, Ireland.

Bible quotations are reproduced from the *Good News Bible* by permission of the Bible Society.

CONTENTS

INTRODUCTION

This book may be your guide to a fascinating, inward journey that will take you no further than God who, for those who want God as a friend, lives within. On the way to God-awareness, you will be invited to experience deep relaxation of body and mind. Your senses will become more perceptive; you will have a new and heightened appreciation of many wonderful things that are going on both within you and round about you. You will be challenged to grow in your knowledge and love of God. If you accept this challenge, you will be changed for the better.

Begin by asking yourself, 'Where am I now?' It may at first seem like a silly question, but go beyond your body to ask the question in regard to your mind and heart, and your feelings. If you find that you are somewhat anxious and fearful about your job because of some planned restructuring announced recently at work, or you are feeling guilty because of the rash words you spoke to your mother over the weekend, or you are definitely not looking forward to that dental appointment tomorrow morning, then it is quite likely that your mind is not in the living room at all, but at the office instead, or in your mother's house, or in the dentist's chair. If your heart is set on next summer's vacation, or on a loved one who is away for a time, then the chances are that a big part of your feelings center around that place or person. Or if you have not eaten in several hours, some part of you is already in the kitchen, at the refrigerator.

That restless feeling, that sense of being scattered and unfulfilled that I seem to experience most of the time may simply be a sign that I am not quite 'together'. Like a broken plate lying on the floor, my life may be in some sense divided into different sections that are not connected as they should be. I live in one part of town, rush across the city every day to work, while my heart is somewhere else entirely. Almost as soon as I sit down with someone, I get distracted. I cannot be wholly present to them—or indeed to myself. My head is full of facts, yet I find it difficult to concentrate. My body and my mind seem to be leading separate lives. I live in a confusing, even threatening, world—or am I the one who is hostile and unreconciled to the neighbours, environment, and indeed, myself?

Body-mind meditation can help you become a more integrated, balanced person. It is an especially helpful approach to meditation if the pace of life is too fast, or if you find yourself frequently tense or exhausted. As body-mind implies, this kind of meditation is not something that goes on only in the mind. It will help you live in touch with your body and its vital rhythms such as your breathing and heart-beat. Your over-worked senses will be calmed and rested. Your thinking, emotions, and bodily activities will begin to work in harmony, instead of fighting one another. You will tend to eat and sleep in a healthier way. You will be less at the mercy of negative feelings toward others, and feel more at home with plant, animal, and bird life and many beautiful things in the world around you that you did not notice before. Above all, you will experience a dawning realisation of the Power behind creation as a wise and loving God, indeed a Father, who is gently drawing us, healing us, and leading us into a happiness and a 'peace, which is far beyond human understanding' (*Philippians* 4.7).

HOW TO USE THIS BOOK

Each chapter offers eight body-mind keys to Christian meditation:

- rest
- breath
- body
- place
- sound
- rhythm
- simplicity
- wholeness

These keys can be viewed as ways to open the door to stillness of body and mind, leading to intimacy with God. Several exercises in awareness and meditation are given with each key.

As you read *Body, Mind & Spirit*, you can stop at any point and do any one of these exercises. They do not have to be done in any particular order, though in a few instances you will be referred to an earlier section for some details. Alternately, as with a do-it-yourself hand-book, you can use the Contents pages to go straight to whatever exercise appeals to you. Select and use whatever you can most easily do or what best suits your temperament or need of the moment. Do not feel that you have to cover everything. Indeed, if you can find even one technique that helps you to practise stillness and meditation over a long period, you will have made the best possible use of this book. In the long run it is better to persevere with one method of meditation than to be chopping and changing or looking for diversion. Meditative stillness calls for a steadiness of purpose. Whichever key or exercise is used, the essential point is that it help us arrive at a sense of God's loving presence and God's call to us. From then on we will understand where our meditative journey has its beginning and its ending. In the words of Jesus, 'No one can come to me unless the Father makes it possible to do so' (*John* 6.65).

Key 1: Rest

REST

Has it ever struck you that whatever you are doing — even reading this sentence — you are burning up energy, and often a lot more than you need to? Just observe yourself for a moment, wherever you are — perhaps having a quick 'read' in your lunchbreak, or travelling home in the train or bus, sitting in your easychair or simply propped up in bed, relaxing.

But how relaxed are you really? For the moment, try and identify just one part of you that may still be a little tense. It could be your neck, shoulders, face, stomach or a leg. Could you relax it more? Try it! Here is a simple test.

EXERCISE 1: SPOTTING TENSION

Sit or lie down. Make yourself as comfortable as you can. Think about your body. Check how it really is. Turn your thoughts to your left leg. Think just about that leg. Close your eyes and picture it. Get the 'feel' of your leg — what is your leg feeling just now? Are you aware of any tense muscles? Is it in a position that is comfortable enough for it to relax? If not, then just move it slowly for a while and experiment with different positions until you find one that is restful, in which it is possible for it to be more relaxed. Go on thinking about and sensing your left leg for a minute or two. Now turn your attention away from your left leg and over to your right one. Notice the difference — how much more uncomfortable your right leg is compared to your left.

This exercise shows some of the hidden tension that 'lives' in our bodies. Muscles that are supposed to be 'off duty' are not in fact, switched off. They are under stress, and are drawing off physical and nervous energy.

Therefore, we often suffer from unnecessary stress, fatigue and irritability. This leaves us restless and lacking harmony in our lives.

For some people, tension can build up into a really vicious cycle that can almost bring their lives to a stand-still. Many diseases, including today's main killers — cancer and cardiac illness — may possibly be linked to deep tensions in people's lives. Certainly, 70% to 80% of minor ailments are known to be stress related. Many people have never experienced real relaxation in their whole lives. The more deep-seated the tension, the more difficult it is to 'let go' and be at ease. But when it is achieved, it is such a benefit and worth all the effort.

The good news is that within a very short time, anyone can learn to completely relax their body. The techniques are simple and I have used them successfully for more than ten years with thousands of people — men and women, old as well as young, including sick people, sufferers from high blood pressure and others. No more than fifteen to thirty minutes was required to achieve deep relaxation for the overwhelming majority — and that sometimes in groups as large as a hundred. Others have been able to learn some of these methods by means of audio cassettes. If you would like to learn to relax, then why not do some of the exercises given in this book?

These exercises are not just about the body, but involve the mind as well. A tense body does not exist on its own. It is always found together with a tense mind. Just think about what happens when you are frightened or angry or frustrated — the rapid heart-beat, knotted stomach, the tightening in your throat.

Your body is like a map of your spirit. If you want to know what is happening in your mind, your emotions, your innermost being — then just look at and become aware of your body. A calm body is an indication that your spirit is calm. An agitated, uneasy, restless body may well be an inner cry for help. That body will refuse to relax until you are willing to look at what is troubling your mind.

Why not allow your body to 'speak' to you about your deeper needs? It will take a little time to understand what the different signals coming through your body might mean. If you are suffering from migraine or eye strain, you might be tempted to reach for the tablets or make arrangements to have your lenses changed. These steps may be necessary, but only as short-term answers. Learning 'body-speak' means being prepared to ask yourself questions, particularly 'why' questions. Why am I getting these migraine headaches, eye strain, stomach ache, back ache or head colds? Why is my throat sore for the past few days? Why am I exhausted now?

Every one of us comes under strong pressure at different times during our lives. It might be money problems, unemployment, worries about our health or a bereavement. Perhaps it is associated with stages in our development such as adolescence, facing examinations. looking for a job, marriage or retirement. Most of us are upset by pressure or hostility from others. Whatever might be causing it, the stress is first taken in by our mind. As we realise its negative character, we experience shock, pain, anger or disappointment in our spirit. We may be conscious of the set-back for only a short time. Nonetheless, it can remain on indefinitely at a deeper, sub-conscious level. It will also register in some way in our body. The pressure or distress that we undergo will look especially for a weak or sensitive zone through which to express itself. In this way many forms of illness can develop that are associated with key areas or centres of consciousness in our body. Tensions seem to build up in one or more of seven particular points or centres in our body.

The *centres* are sensitive zones within the body that respond to what is happening in our mind, heart or spirit. Whenever our mood changes, when we become conscious of something new and significant, when we succeed or fail, are happy or sad — all of this is read in detail by one or more of the *centres*, each of which is a complex bundle of emotional and nervous energy. As we go on to list them just pause and allow yourself to *feel* what is happening at this moment in each one.

EXERCISE 2: CENTRE AWARENESS

Head Centre: begin by sitting or lying down comfortably. Close your eyes and bring your attention to your *head*

15

centre. This is at the very top of your head and the area round and immediately below it. You might like to think

of a series of parallel circles on the skull (like lines of latitude), getting larger but weaker as you move down from the crown. Be aware of any feelings on the surface of your head — and then inside the head. Note the places where the feelings are pleasant — and the places where there is pain or discomfort. Head-colds, migraine and dizziness are among the more common ailments located at this centre. If you are at this moment suffering in the head, then relax and deliberately allow the pain to *be* for a little while. Actually 'surrendering' to a minor pain or ache may rob it of some of its sting.

Eye Centre: the *eye centre* is located round a point mid-way between the two eyes. Close your eyes and relax for

a moment. Then slowly open your eyes and gaze on any small object — even a word on this page. You are now looking . . . but where is the 'you' that is looking? You will discover that the conscious 'looker' that is you, is situated within your head slightly behind your eyes. Experience yourself as 'being there' looking out through your eyes. Do not strain to see anything. Simply remain still and allow the object to show itself to you. Try not to think . . . your conscious self is right now at your *eye centre.* Or, to put in another way, your *eye centre* is 'awake'.

Throat Centre: have you ever felt that your throat had gone dry and closed up? That your Adam's apple was in a hard lump? Relax now and try to focus on the *throat centre* — a very sensitive area the size and shape of a tomato, just below the Adam's apple. Take a few moments to 'locate' yourself within it. As you remain calmly aware of this centre  you will sense your throat becoming less rigid and more open. Pay attention to your breath as it passes in and out through this *centre.*

Heart Centre: move down now to the level of your chest. The *heart centre* occupies a much larger area that might be likened to a small football. Once again become conscious of what is going on within it, and particularly around the heart itself. At one time in my life I used to experience a 'tightening' sensation round my heart. This feeling was telling me that I was under  some stress that was registering in my *heart centre.* It is wise to heed these messages and slow down a little.

Solar Plexus Centre: you will identify the next centre of consciousness quite easily. The *solar plexus centre* may be thought of as a dough-nut shaped band about six inches across that

encircles the navel or belly button. It is the source of our breathing. As you exhale think of your breath as a stream of air beginning at the navel and flowing upwards through your chest, throat and head. As it comes out through your nostrils it becomes one with the great 'ocean' of air. Inhaling reverses the process. Stay with your breathing — *be* at that *centre* for a while.

Pelvic Centre: the *pelvic centre* is located at the genital area. It is there that the biological sex urge is concentrated.

Root Centre: a little below the *pelvic centre*, between genitals and anus, is the *root centre*, an area we are most conscious of during evacuation.

In a very real sense, we live through our *centres*, yet many people are not even aware that these exist. By means of simple awareness exercises, it is possible to become much more conscious of these *centres*, and so relax them and save energy. All you need do is sit quietly in any comfortable position, preferably with your back straight. Close your eyes and bring your mind to any one of your *centres*. Allow whatever feelings that are there to speak to you. At first you may find that you have no feelings at all. But if you continue with the practice, you will learn that the area you are sensing is alive with sensations. Further practice will enable you to focus on tiny particles of your body anywhere at all — in every one of which there are multitudes of sensations waiting to be discovered. Just think of what happens when the point of a pin touches your skin! Our body is like a vast continent, with millions of nerve endings that it uses to communicate with us. That communication *is* sensation. If we do not listen to the message our spirit is sending us via one or other of the body *centres*, we run the risk of damaging that particular zone in our body. And this is where we must look in the first instance for the causes of constipation, ulcers, many forms of stomach upset, heart trouble and other ailments.

Body awareness is not only about avoiding diseases. It also means being prepared to hear what my spirit, my innermost being is trying to say to me. It is about understanding and improving myself. Relaxation and self awareness will help free me from the tension that saps my energy. If there are draughty windows in my house and the roof is not insulated, I will certainly feel cold and uncomfortable in the winter. And within a couple of months my heating bill will bring home to me in concrete terms the cost of that waste — the things I might have bought with the money which now I cannot afford. So it is with my body. As I learn to stop the waste of physical and nervous energy through relaxation, I can begin to dream of new possibilities for my life. I will feel better and more confident to face new undertakings.

EXERCISE 3: DEEP RELAXATION MEDITATION

The following exercise involves physical and mental relaxation, centring or focusing the mind and a meditation on the love of God. It is the experience of this love that makes it possible for us to feel taken care of, to trust, to let go — in a word, to relax.

Take your time with the following sequence of directions. Wearing loose, comfortable clothing lie flat on your back on the floor, arms a bit apart from your sides, your feet about ten to fifteen inches apart. You

19

may place a rug or sleeping bag beneath you, but it is preferable not to do this exercise in bed. Your bed may be just a little too soft to allow your body to lie quite straight and to rest naturally. If you find lying on your back too uncomfortable, then lie on your front. If you have difficulty lying down at all, then sit in whatever position is most comfortable. Do however, try to keep your back fairly upright. It is important that the room be quite warm because, when one relaxes deeply, the body temperature tends to drop. Before you begin, remove shoes, glasses, watch and heavier jewellery.

As you lie there, look down along your body and check that it is in a straight line, not curving to the right or to the left. Stretch your heels along the floor away from your body, your toes towards you — and relax. Slowly roll your head from side to side a few times, leaving it in the most restful position. Expand the fingers of both hands to form stars, stretch — and relax. Become aware of the weight of your body . . . and the points of contact between your body and the floor. Close your eyes and become aware of your breathing, noting its speed . . . its depth.

Bring your attention to your left arm. Slowly raise the entire arm about an inch off the floor. Hold it there for a few seconds. Then, as slowly as you can, lower your arm to the ground and relax. Next turn your attention to the right arm, raising and lowering it in exactly the same slow way.

The sequence of awareness-raising-holding-lowering-relaxing is likewise applied to your left leg . . . right leg . . . head and neck. Go through it all as slowly as you can, all the time making sure that you are completely rested after each stage, before moving on to the next one. After you have lowered your head, rest yourself totally for a few moments. Are you sufficiently warm? If not, then put something over you. Feel free to make minor adjustments in your clothing and position as you prepare to move on to a deeper level of physical relaxation.

Points to remember

RELAXING ARMS, LEGS, NECK

1. Lie comfortably

2. Become aware of the limb

3. Slowly raise it about an inch

4. Hold there for a moment

5. Lower slowly to the ground

6. Relax

Once more bring your attention to your left arm. This time you will not be lifting the arm. Nevertheless, slowly tense the same muscles that you used before. Concentrate on what you are doing, gradually increase the tension in the muscles, building up to a maximum. Consciously hold the tension for a few seconds. Then, as slowly as you can, ease back on the tension, releasing slowly and relaxing the arm completely. When you have rested turn your attention to the right arm and repeat the procedure. In your own time do the same for the muscles of the left leg . . . right leg . . . neck. The sequence this time round is: awareness-tensing-holding-releasing-relaxing. And as before, the more slowly it is done, the better.

Become aware next of the main areas of your body, checking to see where there may be hidden tension. Survey your lower abdomen . . . stomach . . . around the heart . . . throat . . . behind the eyes . . . shoulders . . . back. . . . If you discover any tension, then deal with it by first *increasing* it, bringing it to a maximum, holding it for a moment; and then slowly easing back on the tension, releasing and relaxing. When you are satisfied that your body is deeply relaxed, you can move on to relaxing your mind.

RELAXING ANY MUSCLES

1. Sit or lie down

2. Become aware of tension

3. Slowly *increase* the tension

4. Hold the tension

5. Slowly release tension

6. Relax.

If you find your concentration being upset by some distraction, anxiety or concern, do not push it away from your mind. If you do, it will simply return, probably even more intensely. Instead, hold the distracting thought in front of your mind, at arm's length. Gaze on it in a detached way. Do not analyse it or, if it is a problem in your life, do not try to solve it. Simply be aware of it there, calmly noting its existence. Hold it there in the one spot for some time, not letting it slip away. Then, when you are ready, release it, relax and allow it to float away. Should it return or should another distraction take its place, then deal with it in exactly the same way.

We now move on to centring the mind. Picture in your imagination a square, straight in front of you. It can be any colour and made of any material whatever. Inside the square there is a circle, the circle being slightly smaller than the square and not touching it. Inside the circle there is an equilateral triangle pointing upwards,

22

smaller than the circle and not touching it. Let your mind rest on the figure of square contain-ing circle con-taining triangle. Slowly move to-wards the figure, observing it grow larger as you approach it. Now veer to the

left until you are just outside the left side of the square.

Study the side of the square closely. What colour is it? What is it made out of? What texture? Put your hand out and touch it — note what it feels like . . . Pass through the side of the square, so that you are inside the square but outside the circle, and rest there. Turn your attention next to the circle, noting what it is like to look at and to touch. Pass through into the circle, remaining outside the triangle and pause there. Finally, go through the same procedure with the triangle, passing through one of its sides right into the centre of the figure. Relax there com-pletely. Feel yourself protected by the triangle inside the circle inside the square. The triangle with its three sides is a symbol of the Trinity, one God but three persons – the Father, the Son and the Holy Spirit. Listen now to the words of love that Jesus, the Son of God, is speaking to you:

'Do not be worried and upset — believe in God and believe also in me' (*John* 14.1).

'Know that I am in my Father and that you are in me, just as I am in you' (*John* 14.20).

'Peace is what I leave with you; it is my own peace that I give you. I do not give it as the world does. Do not be worried and upset; do not be afraid' (*John* 14.27).

'Remain united to me, and I will remain united to you' (*John* 15.4).

'I love you just as the Father loves me; remain in my love' (*John* 15.9).

During this part of the meditation, you may spend as little or as long as you like reflecting on any or all of these gospel texts. Allow some time after your reflection just to be there with the Lord, receiving his love and resting in it. This is the most important part of the entire exercise, when you have let go of your own efforts and are passive before (and indeed within) your God. He loves and takes care of us, not because we have earned it in any way, but simply because he is pure Goodness. At this moment, our relaxation of body and mind is an expression of our faith. As St Paul in *Ephesians* puts it: 'It is by grace that you have been saved, through faith; not by anything of your own, but by a gift from God.'

When you are ready to conclude the exercise, move slowly away from the centre of the triangle. Pass slowly in turn out through the triangle . . . the circle . . . the square. Withdraw slowly from the figure, observing it becoming smaller . . . still smaller . . . and eventually disappearing. Become aware of the fact that you have been meditating. Become aware of your body, of how heavy and relaxed it feels. Take note of your breathing, of how slow, how smooth and how deep it has become. Begin to move your fingers and toes . . . your hands and feet. Raise your arms above your head and stretch. Bring your arms down and roll over on one side or the other. Spend a little time resting in silence.

Key 2: Breath

BREATH

Freezing fog billows into the path of our head-lights as we motor through the January darkness. Sitting silently in the back seat, I am acutely aware that my feet are cold, and getting more so with every passing mile. If only I could get out and run or walk for a few minutes — but politeness will not allow me to make that demand on my hosts. I will just have to suffer the numbling cold for the rest of our 130 mile  journey. Then a memory stirs . . . 'The mind, the breath and the body working together are very powerful'. Having nothing else to do but sit there in the cold, I decide to experiment.

I notice that my right leg is a tiny bit colder than my left, so I use my breath to warm it. I relax, closing my eyes and begin to think of my breathing. As I inhale, I imagine light and warmth entering my lungs and spreading out into my body. Exhaling I picture a stream of warmth moving down my right leg and into my foot and toes. Continuing for a few minutes, I *will* that foot to become warm, and at the same time imagine the warming taking place. Now I relax and check the actual situation. And yes, my right foot is now distinctly warmer than the left! Next, focusing on my left leg, I repeat the exercise and find I can warm my left foot so that it is once again a little warmer than the right. Within fifteen minutes both feet are comfortably warm and remain that way until we reach our destination.

This incident is just one example of using a power that exists, usually unrecognised, in each one of us — the power of the breath.

A more dramatic example, familiar to us on our television screens, is the karate expert who halves a solid piece of timber with the side of his hand. This power is not just about deep breathing — the breath can achieve little by itself. It needs to be directed by the mind. Why not try out this power within yourself next time you have difficulty opening a glass jar? Hold the jar in one hand and the lid in the other. Relax all your muscles. Close your eyes and become aware of your breathing. Wait till the breathing has really slowed down. Now visualise the lid becoming loose and moving. Hold that image of the jar opening and the next time you begin to exhale apply as much force as you can to the jar and the lid. The result may surprise you, especially if you are not usually very successful opening stiff lids.

Using the power of the breath means first of all getting in touch with one's breathing. A big problem here is the way we learned (at least in western countries) how we should breathe. The tummy was to be held well in. A tummy expanded, filled with air did not seem to fit in with the ideal of a slim, trim waist-line. And just in case we forgot this: girdles, belts, tight trousers or skirts ensured that deep abdominal breathing simply could not take place. European clothing and culture does permit and indeed prizes chest expansion — just think of the ads for body-building courses. Yet even here the emphasis is on 'dynamic tension' rather than on breathing based on relaxation.

The breath, as life itself, is God-given. Before we can make proper use of it, we must first *accept it as a gift*. We need to allow it to flow freely, rather than try to dominate it. If we can simply relax totally and let go, we will find that our breathing, left to itself, will gradually slow down, deepen and become calm. See it for yourself in the following exercise.

EXERCISE 4: ALLOWING THE BREATH

Lie flat on the floor, arms by your side and with your feet slightly apart. Relax, close your eyes and become aware of your breathing. Just think about the air coming in and going out through your nostrils — do *not* control it. Surrender to the smooth flow of air. Note the cool sensation in your nostrils as you inhale — the warm sensation as you exhale. If you discover that tight clothing, a belt, a watch or jewellery is restricting your breathing, quietly adjust or remove it. See if you can learn how your body reacts to the breath. First, think about your abdomen; next, the rib cage and finally, the top of your chest. Observe any movement, any expansion that might occur in your stomach, ribs or chest. Above all, do not hold in your stomach. Neither should you force it out. This is an occasion for letting go of muscular controls and letting things happen. It is as if you are not so much breathing as being breathed. With each *inhalation* God is giving you a priceless gift: life. Do not grab at it — just accept it, receive it thankfully, allow it to be. Imagine that God is embracing you with the breath — his breath, your breath. As you go on with the exercise, you may notice that when you breathe in, your entire body seems more full of air than ever before. This is quite normal. If it seems strange at first, that could be because you may have been unconsciously cutting off your breathing for many years through tension and wrong thinking about how you are supposed to breathe.

Stay relaxed and enjoy that new freedom to breathe fully and the sense of peace that comes with it. Understand that full breathing is not something that we can earn or take by force. It is given freely to those who can receive it.

'Allowing the breath' is not just a new and richer rhythm of lung expansion and contraction. It is also a statement of the spirit. By allowing myself to *inhale* freely and fully, I am saying with my body that I accept my life whole-heartedly. I am happy to be alive at this moment. As you relax and slowly draw in the life-giving breath, you might like to ponder the very last line from the *Book of Psalms*: 'All living, breathing creatures, praise the lord.' Repeat this phrase in your imagination. Allow the words to be absorbed into the breath until the movement of your lungs, diaphragm and chest becomes a kind of 'body-hymn' of praise and thanks to God for the gift of your life.

The deeply relaxing movement of *exhalation*, on the other hand, expresses trust, or a willingness to let go. It invites me to breathe out my spirit, to surrender my life to the God who gives it to me in the first place. The extent to which I am able to set my out-breath free, reflects in some way my willingness to hand my life over to the Lord. Anxiety, fear or a traumatic experience may have paralysed a person's spirit. They will also have distorted the natural flow of his breathing, making it tense, shallow and uneven. And yet the breath, while it mirrors the soul's condition, can also be used to help it find healing and renewed faith. Here is a simple breathing meditation that can help re-build and strengthen your trust in a loving God.

EXERCISE 5: BREATH MANTRA

Wearing loose, warm clothing lie flat on a sleeping bag, rug or thin mattress. That is the best arrangement, though if you find it too uncomfortable, you may lie on a bed or sit comfortably. Take some time to get your body relaxed, making use (if you like) of the technique given at the start of exercise 3 in the last chapter. Then, fully relaxed and with your eyes closed, turn your attention to your breathing, observing it coming in and going out through your nostrils. Take note of any tension that may be in your body, but don't consciously get rid of it or even judge it. Just calmly become aware of the breath. How fast/slow? How shallow/deep? How jerky/smooth? Resist any temptation to be critical of yourself or of your breathing. Be a neutral observer. Next, bring before your mind the words: 'Into your hands, Lord, I commend my spirit.'

This prayer is based on Psalm 31: 5. It was the prayer of Jesus as he hung on the cross (*Luke* 23.46). They were in fact his last words and with them he surrendered his earthly life to God his Father. As you lie there, repeat these words to yourself a number of times, allowing them to sink in.

Now, bring your attention back to your breathing. Focus on your *in*halation. As you inhale, think about the words 'into your hands, Lord'. Continue to do this for five or six inhalations at least. As you go on, fit the words to the length of your in-breath. Do *not* in any way adjust your breathing to the words. Only when you sense that your in-breath and the words 'into your hands, Lord' have been moulded together, should you turn your

30

attention to the *ex*halation. This time take the words 'I commend my spirit' and fit them to the out-breath. When these likewise have been moulded into one, put the two sets of words together and match them with the complete cycle of inhalation and exhalation.

As you practise this for some time, you will find that your breath is in a sense 'speaking' the words for you — 'Into your hands, Lord, I commend my spirit.'

And remember: do not force your breathing.

As you become more practised at this exercise, you may like to start visualising. Bring before your mind any familiar image of God — Jesus in some Gospel scene or, best of all, on the cross as he prayed these words. Allow your breath and words to become your prayer. If you wish, focus on part of the phrase, for instance 'I commend my spirit'. Each time you repeat these words breathing out, sense yourself as really commending or committing yourself to God: trusting him and putting yourself entirely in his hands.

EXERCISE 6: CREATION MEDITATION

There are many other bible texts that can be meditated on by means of this method of relaxed aware breathing. Lying on the floor in the same way, you can bring to mind the text about the creation of man from *Genesis* 2.7: 'Then the Lord God took some soil from the ground and formed a man out of it; he breathed life-giving breath into his nostrils and the man began to live.' As you breathe out, let go completely and imagine that your body is melting into the ground. With each exhalation visualise yourself progressively merge with and dissolve into the earth. Allow the particles of your body to separate and become one with the soil of the earth.

Relax totally for a few moments.

Now shift your attention from your exhalation to the inhalation. Reflect on the words '(the Lord) breathed life-giving breath into his nostrils' as you breathe in. Continue with this for a few minutes and, as you do, begin to visualise God breathing into your nostrils as you inhale. With each breath gratefully draw in the life that God is giving you. Go on then to imagine in addition particles of earth coming together bit by bit to make up your body. Include in your reflection the words 'the Lord God took some soil from the ground and formed a man out of it.' Continue to picture your body being formed from the earth and with each inhalation slowly emerging out of the ground. Finally, to the words 'the man began to live', lie there calmly breathing in and breathing out, conscious of the life that God has put within you.

Be gentle with yourself as you do this and the previous meditation. Do not feel that you have to go through all the different stages at one go. As you lie there, always take time to ensure that you are relaxed totally. Allow your lungs, rather than your mind, to do the praying. When you have decided to stop meditating, once again observe your breathing. As compared with the beginning of the exercise, has it become any slower, smoother or deeper? Do you find yourself more relaxed, at peace or ready to trust? Do you have a greater sense of the presence of a loving God, than when you started?

The above exercises (4, 5 and 6) involve the breath and the spirit working together. They can be very soothing to both soul and body. The next exercise can in addition be of direct benefit to other people.

EXERCISE 7: HEALING BREATH

As you relax (preferably lying down) and become aware of your breathing, reflect on the words 'Holy

32

Spirit' as you inhale; and 'give me your love' as you exhale. Take time as before to allow the words to become matched with the timing of your breathing. Let the complete phrase 'Holy Spirit, give me your love' become part of you, just as your breath is part of you. Make sure that you are fitting the words to the natural rhythm of your breathing, and not your breathing to the words.

Keep on mentally repeating the words as you breathe, until your reach the stage where you are able to relax and 'hear' the prayer continuing with the breath without any further effort on your part.

Now centre your attention on your inhalation and the words 'Holy Spirit'. As you breathe in, picture the air flowing smoothly in through your nostrils, down the wind-pipe and filling the lungs.

Be aware of whatever sensations — cool, ticklish, etc. — are created by the air as it moves down.

Recall the gospel scene from *John* 20.19 —23 where the risen Jesus breathes on the disciples and says: 'receive the Holy Spirit'. You might like to imagine the Lord saying these words to you as he breathes on you. As he breathes out, draw in his breath and the Spirit that he is offering you. With each inhalation draw in his love . . . his peace . . . his healing . . . his joy.

Really *feel* these qualities growing within you as your lungs fill up with air. Stay with this movement for as long as you like. Surrender to it. Enjoy what the Lord in his love is giving to you.

Relax completely.

If you would like to go further, you can turn your attention to the out-breath and the words 'give me your love'. As you exhale, imagine the Spirit and his gifts spreading throughout your body: up to the top of your head . . . out to your fingers, down to your feet and toes. Give particular attention to any part of your body that may be injured or unwell. Spend some time directing the Spirit's healing power into that area with the words 'give me your *healing*'. Be very passive and open to whatever God might want to do with you during that time. Be sensitive to any feelings of warmth, of calmness or of energy that you may have anywhere in your body.

Finish off as before with a short period of quiet rest.

Your out-breath can also be directed in a loving way towards other people. As you relax, bring to mind any person that you love or care for, and whom you would like to pray for at this moment.

Again meditating on the words (adapted slightly) 'give him/her (or name) your love . . . peace . . . healing . . . joy', allow them to merge with your exhalation.

Concentrate first on matching words to breath. Only when they have once more become part of you should you go on to visualising the person.

This entails forming a mental picture of the person. Note him or her in as much detail as possible — position, clothing, surroundings, facial expression. Allow yourself to hear his or her voice and if you like, stretch out your hand and touch him or her. Holding the image, again become conscious of your breathing and the words that you have moulded in the out-breath. If the person being prayed for is sick, it would be very appropriate to use the words 'give him/her your healing'. Maintain your contact with the image of that person and with your breathing.

As you exhale, breathe out your love towards that person. Do not strain as you do it. Remain quite serene and allow your breath in its own way and according to its own rhythm express your care, your concern and your love. Remember, love is not something that should be forced. Instead, if I can become peaceful within myself and become the real 'I' that God wants me to be, love for others will tend to flow out of me gently and without fuss. Even if the person being prayed for is one whom I find it difficult to love, or who has hurt me in some way, this form of meditation will help heal and soften my attitude, provided I am willing to surrender myself to the Holy Spirit that I was asking for in the meditation based on the in-breath and the words 'Holy Spirit'. Besides, this prayer is not so much a question of my love for the person, as God's love for him or her. The extraordinary truth is that God wants to love that person through me, and perhaps even to heal him/her through me.

This type of prayer can be used for all kinds of human need — healing for the sick, peace and reconciliation for individuals and nations, joy to the sorrowing or depressed, courage for those who are fearful or anxious, truth, faith and love to all.

Nor need this prayer be limited to the living. It is good to pray for the dead, particularly members of our own family tree. We can visualise them as we remember them in life or from a photograph. To our out-breath we can match the words 'give him/her (or name) your peace/rest'.

Taking your prayer for another a stage further, you might visualise the person *changing* as a result of prayer. 'See' the sick person becoming healthy, the angry, resentful one becoming calm, the distressed being filled with peace and joy. This kind of visualisation is a statement of hope. We believe in the power of sincere prayer. Above all, we believe in God's goodness and power to make good things happen. This is not to say that the person prayed for will be improved exactly as we picture him or her (though this might indeed happen!). We can be certain however, that good will always result from prayer based on firm faith, as Jesus promised: 'Ask, and you will receive; seek, and you will find; knock, and the door will be opened to you' (*Matthew* 7.7).

Points to remember

1. Relax completely at the start of each exercise

2. *Observe*, but *do not control* your breathing

3. Make your mantra fit the pattern of breathing, and not *vice versa*

4. 'Hear' your breath sounding the words

5. Visualise

6. Relax

Key 3: Body

KEY 3: BODY

About twice a week I try to find time to visit my local sports centre. In the gym there I spend a few minutes on each of the different pieces of apparatus — cycling and rowing machines, bench and various weight apparatus. I don't do anything too strenuous — just work at a rhythm and speed and weight that allows me to enjoy the work-out. A few leisurely lengths of the swimming pool nearby completes my routine. I leave feeling good both physically and mentally. Physical exercise is not only a vital ingredient of bodily health; it also helps one to cope with depressive moods, bad temper, mental fatigue and inability to concen- 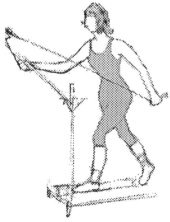 trate. A certain level of body fitness and flexibility can be a great help to meditation.

Have you noticed how even a simple walk can clear your head and allow your thoughts to flow more easily? If you are more energetic, you get the same result through cycling, swimming, jogging or a keep-fit sequence. Games like golf, squash, tennis or bowls may not work quite so well because one's thoughts are directed towards the objective of winning.

Any physical activity which is done in silence is an excellent preparation for meditation. Very likely you get many opportunities throughout the day for such activities, for example, house tidying, working in your garden or simply walking to the shops. Quite apart from making your body fit for meditation, any of the above kinds of activity can themselves become a form of meditation, provided it is done in the right spirit. Here is an exercise for the next time you are left on your own to do the washing-up.

EXERCISE 8: WASHING-UP MEDITATION

Decide first of all that you are going to *enjoy* doing this work!

Look calmly on the cups, plates, dishes and sauce-pans piled in the sink.

Deliberately see them not as a boring nuisance, but as an actual opportunity to focus mentally and to grow spiritually.

Having checked that the transistor radio is switched off, start by becoming aware of what you are doing — emptying out the remains of food or tea, opening the hot tap, inserting the stopper.

Feel the water as it changes from cool to warm to hot.

Note the sensation as you rub the cloth over each piece of crockery.

Be convinced that what you are doing now is the most important, the most absorbing, activity in the world. Do not think about how long the work is likely to take, or how many more items are left to be washed.

Be totally present to that saucer you are now drying with the tea-towel. Be totally content in what you are doing.

Forget about the past and the future. Instead be fully present and alive *now*, at the present moment — the only time that is truly real.

EXERCISE 9: WORK AS PRAYER

When you have practised this kind of domestic activity meditation a few times, you may like to take things a stage further. Begin with a moment's silence. Remind yourself that what you are about to do is the right thing for you at this time, that it is a service, an expression of love for others, that it is what God wants you to be doing right now. Within your heart dedicate the work to God. The *Book of Proverbs* (16.3) tells us: 'Ask the Lord to bless your plans, and you will be successful in carrying them out.'

You may like to pray mentally in your own words along the lines of: 'Lord, I want to do this work for love of you and of others. Help me do it as perfectly as possible.'

As you work, remind yourself from time to time of what you are doing, why you are doing it and for whom. All of this may seem like making too much out of washing a few dishes or some other simple task. Yet it is the spirit in which you work that counts. And when the job is done, you will be left, not just with clean dishes, but with a somewhat changed you.

The craftsmen who worked on the great mediaeval cathedrals worked in this spirit of faith and dedication. The work they left behind them reflects a sense of the beauty and peace of God. In today's world we need to get away from the idea that all human work has its price in money and time, and apart from that, has little meaning or value.

The simpler and less prestigious forms of work are the very ones that can most easily be turned into prayer.

Painting a fence, pushing a lawn-mower or a floor-sweeper around, cleaning windows or a room are jobs which are not intellectually demanding. On the job-market they would be classified as 'lower paid'. Yet, because of their very simplicity, when one is doing them, one's mind and spirit can be freed from the tangled patterns of thinking which sometimes get between us and God. The bodily exertion, the activities of seeing and touching simple uncomplicated matter, helps us to purify our senses and to get into contact with simple material things. How otherwise would one really look at and touch a piece of rough wood or a pane of glass?

Over many centuries and in different parts of the world, particular forms of exercise have been developed both to prepare the body for meditation and to be in fact themselves meditation. The slow motion movements of T'ai Chi Chuan, which many Chinese practise out of doors each morning, promote good health but also lead to quietness of mind. Religious dance is found in Hinduism and in many parts of the Islamic world. Yoga is perhaps the best-known kind of bodily activity that can be used as a form of meditation.

When I get up in the morning an hour earlier than the rest of the household, I go through a series of yoga postures for about half-an-hour. I follow this up with another half-hour's sitting meditation. The easy stretching and bending of yoga makes it much easier for me to sit in stillness. Indeed, the main purpose for which yoga postures were developed, over the past two thousand years plus, was to prepare the body for long periods of meditation. And these exercises have certainly enabled me to sit comfortably still without having my mind disturbed by aches, 'pins and needles' and tiredness. In addition to this, I have been able to use some yoga postures as a kind of body language for prayer.

EXERCISE 10: POSTURES FOR PRAYER

If you would like to do some simple yoga exercises as a way of praying, then you will need some space in a warm but airy carpeted room. Wear loose, light clothing, such as a track suit. Remove your watch, glasses or contact lenses, and larger items of jewellery. Exercising should be done on an empty stomach and at a time when you are less likely to be disturbed — this might mean creeping down to the sitting-room while the rest of the family are still asleep.

Begin by lying flat on your back on the floor. If you wish, you may place a rug or a sleeping bag underneath you, but do not use a pillow. Just lie there for a while, your feet about twelve inches apart and your arms slightly away from your sides.

Before doing any exercise, always make sure that you are completely relaxed. Become aware of your breathing, making sure that it is slow and even before you begin.

The second important point is that you be aware of what you are feeling in your body all the time that you are stretching or exerting. Pain is an indication that you are beginning to over-do things. It is your body's way of telling you to go no further. If you remain 'connected' with your body as you practise yoga, then you are very unlikely to hurt or harm yourself in any way. So, no background music, please! And do only as many of the following postures as you yourself find helpful and can do without straining.

BEFORE EXERCISING . . .

1. *Relax* completely

2. Become *aware* of your body

3. Get in touch with your *breathing*

AS YOU EXERCISE . . .

1. No background music

2. Keep in touch with body feelings

3. Remember: pain means you are over-exercising

Corpse Posture: This is simply lying on your back as described above. As you lie there, mentally let go of whatever may be weighing on your mind — distractions,  fears, responsibilities etc. The *New Testament* tells us: 'Leave all your worries with Him (God), because He cares for you' (I *Peter* 5.7). Spend a few minutes thinking about these words and make them a reality for yourself. If things are really difficult in your life, echo in your mind Saint Paul's message of hope, which sustained him in many tribulations: it is 'as though we were dead, but, as you see, we live on' (2 *Corinthians* 6.9). Remember, God is there to help. The sense of this posture reminds us of dying, but also of resurrection and hopefulness.

Forward Bend: Close your eyes and get in touch with your breathing — not controlling but simply observing the air as it enters and leaves your nostrils. Do not begin the exercise until you are satisfied that your breathing is slow and relaxed. Then, on an inhalation raise both your arms up above your head and back onto the floor behind you. As you exhale, bring your arms forward again and raise your  head and shoulders. Stretch forward towards your feet, making sure that you do not bend your knees. Hold on to your feet or, if that is not possible without bending your knees, somewhere along your legs. Remain in this position for a few moments, breathing normally and taking note of the stretching that is taking place in your lower back and at the backs of your knees. Next raise first one buttock and then the other — you will find that this will enable you to reach a little bit further. As you hold this posture, you may find after some time that on an exhalation you are able without strain to reach down even more.

The forward bend is a way of expressing with your body an acceptance of life with its ups and downs.

There is in each one of us a built-in resistance towards some of the things to which God may be calling us. Even

Jesus had great difficulty accepting his rejection, his loss of friends and especially his approaching death.

As you lean forward into this position, you experience your body's resistance to being bent and stretched. Your efforts to overcome this can become a way of symbolising loving acceptance of God and his guidance and the challenges that stretch you.

As you do this posture, you might reflect on the words from the *Book of Psalms* 119.36: 'Bend my heart to obey your law'. Slowly coming out of the forward bend, lie down on your back and relax completely.

Spinal Twist: After you have rested, place both your hands underneath your back and press down on the floor, thus bringing yourself into a sitting position. Bend your right knee and bring it up as close as possible to your chest. Take your right leg in both arms and lift it over the left leg so that your right foot is now on the floor outside your left thigh. Begin now to turn your head and shoulders around to the right. Bring your left elbow to the outside of your right knee, using it to lever 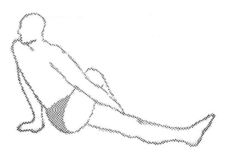 your right leg to the left and your upper body to the right. Put your right hand on the floor behind you for support and to help twist your body further. Turn your head as far around to the right as you can, looking behind you if possible. Hold the position, making sure you are breathing normally and being aware of the twisting sensation in your back. If you find your breathing becoming laboured then come back out of the posture right away.

With practice you may find that you can manoeuvre your left arm so that it reaches down the outside of the right leg and your left hand can even grip the right foot — thus giving you more leverage and enabling you to twist further round. When you feel you have held this posture long enough, slowly turn back to the 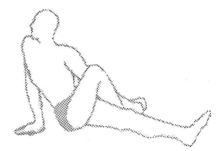 front, straighten your right leg and give it a little shake. Pause for a moment's rest and do exactly the same with the left leg (interchanging 'left' and 'right' in the directions given above).

The spinal twist allows one to experience within one's body the meaning of the word 'turn'. It is an important word in the bible in the sense of 'turning back to God', repentance or change of heart. Attempting to overcome your resistance to physical turning as you perform this posture, why not reflect on one of the relevant passages, for example: 'turn to me now and be saved' (*Isaiah* 45.22). When you have finished with the spinal twist, slowly lie down on your back and relax completely.

Prostration: Now roll over onto your front, place your two hands one on top of the other underneath your

forehead. Rest there in the prostration posture and allow some time for your breath and heart-beat to slow down.

46

This position may be used to express worship of God and may ideally be done in front of an ikon, crucifix or other symbol of God. As you lie there, you may like to reflect on some line from the bible such as: 'In honour of the name of Jesus all beings in heaven, on earth, and in the world below will fall on their knees, and all will openly proclaim that Jesus Christ is Lord, to the glory of God the Father' (*Philippians* 2.10-11).

Cobra: This is an ideal posture for when you are feeling low and crushed. Remove your hands from underneath your forehead and place them by your sides, turning your face either to the right or to the left and relax. Next, place your chin on the ground and become aware of the rhythm of your breathing. As you inhale, slowly raise your head and shoulders as far off the ground as you can. As you begin to exhale, bring your hands up underneath your shoulders and press down against the floor, thus raising your head and shoulders further. Keep your hips on the ground throughout and notice the sensation in your back as you curve upwards. Hold the position for a while breathing normally. Then slowly lower your head and shoulders back onto the ground, place your arms by your sides and relax

47

completely with your head facing to one side for a few breaths, then to the other, and so on as you rest there.

The effort to raise your head, particularly the 'no hands' phase, resembles the arching movement of a cobra – hence the name. The author of *Psalm 22*, the one which begins with the line 'My God, my God, why have you abandoned me?'felt himself so stripped of human dignity that, later on in verse 6, he exclaims: 'I am no longer a man; I am a worm, despised and scorned by everyone!' This psalm was prayed by Jesus as he hung on the cross.

As you do the cobra posture, why not experience in your body, as Jesus did to an extreme degree, what it must actually be like to feel like a worm or a snake?

Pose of a Child: When you have recovered your breath after the cobra, bring yourself up onto all fours. Sit backwards onto your heels, letting your chest come down onto your thighs and your head touch the floor. Bring your arms back behind you until they are just outside your legs. You are now in the restful pose of a child,  which is the same as the foetal position. Hold this posture for a while reflecting on God's words to the Prophet Jeremiah: 'I chose you before I gave you life, and before you were born I selected you . . .' (*Jeremiah* 1.5), or alternately, the words of *Psalm* 131.2: 'As a child lies quietly in its mother's arms, so my heart is quiet within me.'

Forward Bend (standing): Stand up slowly. Have your feet slightly apart, toes pointing forward. Let your arms hang by your sides and, with your head well out of your shoulders, look steadily at some object that is level with your eyes. Get in touch with your breathing and as you begin to inhale, bring your arms out from your sides and up above your head, holding your shoulders well back all the while. Have your hands together with arms straight above your head when you have just filled your lungs. Then, as you begin to exhale, lean forward, bringing your out-stretched arms towards the floor. Make sure that you do not bend your knees. Clasp your feet or, if that is not possible, your legs as far down as you can. Hold the position and breathe normally for a few moments. Then, on an inhalation begin to raise your arms, holding them together and well out in front of your body, palms facing upwards in a lifting movement. Again have your arms directly overhead when you have completed in-haling. As you exhale bring your arms in an outward, backward, downward movement until, at the end of your exhalation, your arms are back by your sides.

In the beginning you may find it difficult to get movement and breath working together. With a little practice, you will find that they will relate to each other naturally almost without thinking about it.

Again, as you practise, be aware of where your body is exerting itself and being stretched. Pay particular attention to the back of the shoulders and upper arms, backs of legs and lower back. This is a good

loosening-up routine for early in the morning.

A simple 'morning offering' prayer can easily be integrated with the forward bend.

As you raise your arms (breathing in) think of the words 'O my God'.

Bend forward and down to the words 'I bow down before you'.

Think of the words 'I offer my life to you' as you come up with your hands in front of you in a lifting movement.

Finally, lower your arms to 'Amen'.

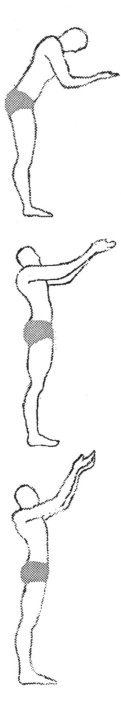

Do this slowly and feel free to use your imagination as you pray with your body. Raising your hands, you might picture something that represents you, your work or your life — for example, food that you will prepare during the day, money that you will earn, or some person that you have difficulty relating with.

Then, as your hands have reached their highest point, you might imagine God receiving your gift, accepting your sorrow and joy.

Should you be fortunate enough to have the rising sun shining in your window as you are getting up, then the above sequence can be performed facing it. The sun marks the beginning of a new day. It is also a symbol of Christ, who brings us the new life of this Resurrection. If however, you have to manage without the sun, you may stand in front of any religious image that reminds you of God and do your forward bend.

EXERCISE 11: BODY PRAYER

As an alternative to the standard postures described above, you may like to express yourself bodily to God in a way that is more free. Come before your 'altar' or religious symbol and try speaking to God through your body in any way that feels right. You can bow, kneel, lie, dance, sway, whirl or use any other way of moving that comes naturally to you. Do not plan beforehand or think about what you will do. Pause and just let your heart reach out to the Lord with love. Then allow your body, rather than your mind or your lips, express your prayer, your gratitude, your joy, your adoration. Let it be as spontaneous and happy as it would be with any human person that you love and respect deeply. Your friendship with God need be no less creative and free than your human friendships.

EXERCISE 12: EYE MANTRA

Take up any comfortable sitting position for some eye exercises. These are designed to relieve eye strain, to relax and tone up the muscles of your eyes and can help to maintain and even improve your sight.

Check that you have removed your glasses or contact lenses!

Before each exercise, let your eyes close lightly and 'palm' them, by holding your cupped hands over them so as to block out the light. At the same time become aware of the groups of muscles around each eye and relax them. Once these are relaxed, you are ready to begin.

Slowly open your eyes and look straight ahead, preferably at some distant fixed object. Without moving your head, look up and down two or three times. Then close your eyes and relax them for a little while, palming them if you find this helpful. Opening your eyes slowly, look right and left a few times. Then close them and relax. When your eyes  are fully rested, open them and look to the top right of your field of vision, then bottom left, top right, bottom left — and rest.

After that do the same for the other arm of the 'x', that is, top left and bottom right.

Relax the eyes completely.

Opening them again, look upwards and move your gaze in a circular path as if reading off the numbers on an enormous clock face just in front of you. When you have completed the circle, close and rest your eyes.

Opening them, repeat the procedure in the reverse direction.

Finally, open your eyes and look into the distance. Gently bring your gaze in to the tip of your nose, and back out again. Do this a number of times and then rest.

These eye exercises can be developed as a form of prayer. With your up/down and left/right movements, you will be tracing the sign of the cross. You can use this eye gesture as a means of expressing your faith in the cross of Jesus. Making the sign of the cross has for centuries been a means whereby Christians have expressed their faith.

The up/down and right/left movements can each be accompanied mentally by any mantra of two syllable, for example, the Holy Name, 'Jesus'. The same is true of each of the 'x' movements.

Any of these movements done twice can be accompanied by any mantra having four syllable, for example, *Maranatha*. Here the sequence would be: up (*ma*) — down (*ra*) — up (*na*) — down (*tha*); and so on.

Always have the timing of the mantra following the natural rhythm of your eye movements, and not the other way round. These same mantras can also be used with the circular movements, again matching syllables to the different steps that your eyes take as they move around the circle, first one way and then the other. Looking alternately into the distance and at the tip of your nose, can likewise be used to time your mantra.

Any of the above series can be repeated several times. Just take care that you do not do them so energetically that you actually strain the eyes. Take time to rest your eyes after each exercise. Palming them is one way of doing this. Another equally effective method is gazing at a single lighted candle in a darkened room.

Key 4: Place

PLACE

Your senses of seeing, hearing, taste, touch and smell can be used to help you meditate. This is most easily done if you have access to any small room where you could have the freedom to create your own environment for meditation, through the use of light and darkness, religious symbols, incense, music (recorded or even sung by yourself), meditation tapes and some very simple furnishings such as a rug and cushion or prayer stool to sit on. Alternately, you could create a temporary prayer-environment (on a daily basis) in any room where you could be undisturbed for an hour.

Here is an example of this kind of meditation approach.

EXERCISE 13: A HOLY PLACE

Check that the curtains in the room are light-tight.

Set up some religious image against the wall at one end. This might be a crucifix or an ikon showing the face of Christ. The important thing is that it be symbolic of what you believe and as such, should be chosen carefully.

Place a candle in front of your symbol. Now light the candle, draw the curtains and sit quietly where you can gaze without straining on the candle-lit image of Christ. This should be slightly lower than eye level — looking down a little is more restful than looking up.

Let your attention be drawn to him who is represented in the ikon or crucifix. Remind yourself that he is God; and that 'God is light, and there is no darkness at all in Him' (I *John* 1.5).

Note the details of the figure of Christ as it is lit up by the flickering flame: his body, his face and above all, his eyes. Think about his love for you and reflect on one or two specific occasions in your life when you have felt his love, his compassion, his peace close to you.

After some time, conclude your analysis of the image and just *be*. Your meditation at this stage is no longer active thinking, something that you *do*. It becomes instead something that you *allow*.

Allow the Lord who is alive and active everywhere in the universe to love you, to heal you, to give you his own peace (see *John* 14.27).

This simple arrangement of ikon and candle can be of great help in getting close to God through your sense of seeing. You can also make use of your sense of smell in this type of meditation by burning a little incense either in stick or granular form. Alternately, you may use an aromatic oil. Smell works powerfully by association. Remember the currant bread our grannies used to bake? If you do, the chances are you remember it by its aroma rather than by its taste. Have a favourite aroma (and the means to produce it) that you will associate with the holy — with God, and that you will use only when you meditate.

How To Create A Prayer Space

If you can, it is worth while taking a little trouble to set aside a special area in your room for meditation. Combine as many elements as you find helpful in the one meditation. For example, apart from an ikon, candle and incense, you might use your cassette-player. In this way sight, sound and smell can work together to create a deeply meditative atmosphere. You may like to furnish the area with a pot plant or a few fresh flowers. A special rug or mat can serve to remind you (and others) that it is a holy place. A very natural follow up to this idea would be the practice of removing your shoes each time you enter the place of prayer, just as Moses did in response to the Lord's command: 'Take off your sandals, because you are standing on holy ground' (*Exodus* 3.5).

THE PLACE FOR MEDITATION

1. Religious symbol with candle, *etc.*

2. Your meditation seat

3. Incense, flowers

4. Sound, recorded or live

5. Your Bible

EXERCISE 14: SITTING

Particular attention needs to be paid to the way you sit when you meditate. The two essentials here are *comfort* and *steadiness*. You will want to be able to sit still throughout your meditation, without being so tortured by discomfort in your legs or back that you will be able to think of nothing else. The classical postures for

meditation are various forms of
cross-legged positions and sitting
back on one's heels. These are
eastern in origin and will not be
easy for the average westerner.
Much less difficult is the use of a
prayer stool. You kneel and
place the stool bridge-like across
your ankles. Then slowly sit back
until you are resting on it. If you
cannot get a prayer stool, you
might try using a cushion in its
place. Again kneel, place the
cushion across your ankles and
sit back.

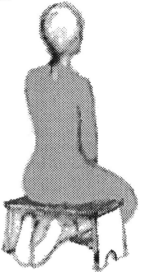

Those who have difficulty with all of the above
methods of sitting can use an ordinary upright chair.
Find one that allows you to sit so that your body forms two
right-angles. If you cannot find such a chair, then any
upright chair can be adapted to suit with the help of a
cushion or folded blanket. If the lower half of your legs
is too long, then use your cushion or blanket to raise the
height of the seat. If your legs are too short for the chair,
place the cushion, blanket or any other suitable object
under your feet. Now sit with your back and your calves
upright. Begin to relax your leg muscles. You may find at
this stage that your knees tend to fall either inwards or
outwards. If inwards, then bring your feet closer
together. If outwards, then separate your feet a little
more. You will soon learn where to place your feet in
such a way that your legs can be upright and relaxed,
without any tendency to fall inwards or outwards.

Now think about your left leg. Is it fully relaxed? Let
your awareness move slowly up and down the leg from
toes right up to the hip. Check each muscle for tension

as you go along. Repeat the process a few times if necessary until you are quite satisfied that your leg is totally at ease.

Bring your mind across to your right leg. Note immediately how much more tense this leg is compared with the one you have been working on. Let your mind move slowly up and down your right leg until it too is completely relaxed.

Think next about the position of your back. It should be fairly upright, though certainly not rigidly so. It might help if you think of your back as made up of thirty-three bones called vertebrae, which when you sit up, rest like bricks one on top of the other. If one leans to the side or front or back, some muscular effort is required just to hold the back in position. This is why, whenever we lounge in an arm-chair, we find that we have to change our position every couple of minutes. On the other hand, when we sit upright, the vertebrae are balanced, like a vertical column of bricks. No effort is required to hold this position steady, and it will be possible to relax our back muscles. In the beginning it may not be that easy, of course, due to the fact that we are so unaccustomed to sitting up straight, without being rigid. Practise sitting upright yet relaxed on your 'prayer chair' whenever you get the opportunity. In time, you will find that you will be able to sit quite still for considerable periods of time. As you practise, think about the muscles of your back. Bring your awareness gently up and down your back a few times, checking that it is relaxed.

Having relaxed your legs and your back, move on next to your arms. With each arm check that it is resting comfortably on your thigh or in your lap. Make sure that it is in a position where it can be totally at rest. Again survey the arm mentally from shoulder to finger-tips, ensuring that there is no tenseness anywhere.

Finally, turn your attention to your head and neck. Gently move your head backwards and forwards, to the left and to the right, taking stiffness out of your neck and at the same time finding the mid-point of balance, where your head can rest on your shoulder without the need to make any effort at all to keep it in place. If you have not already done so, slowly close your eyes and relax your whole body and mind completely.

EXERCISE 15: ART GALLERY MEDITATION

The special place where you meditate need not necessarily be in your home. Some people find it easier to reach stillness in the corner of a quiet church or chapel, or in an art gallery. These buildings sometimes offer profound inspiration to prayer in the form of statues, stained-glass windows or religious paintings. Some years ago, on a visit to the National Gallery of Art in Washington, I was privileged to be able to sit quietly and contemplate the poignant *Crucifixion*, a small painting by Matthis Grunewald, dating from 1510. My gaze was first drawn to the figure of Christ, torn and beaten to a grotesque mass, hanging from a cross-beam that seemed ready to snap under the weight — the head crowned and the body torn by long thorns. Then on to the grieving Virgin Mary and Apostle John standing on either side, and the kneeling Magdalen at Christ's feet. Behind the cross, blackness — black sun, black sky, black greenish-brown landscape. I found myself staying on, in a paradox of fascinated revulsion, picking out additional details in the painting; for example, the unnatural bluish-green colour of Christ's skin. I observed how the heads of the four people in the painting marked the angles of a square, balanced on one of its corners; and how Christ's twisted arms seemed to be extensions of the two upper-most sides of the square. I asked myself what kind of God could allow himself to be shown in such an absurd light — in fact *be* in the absurd position that I could see before me. The words of *Isaiah* 52.14 came to my mind: 'Many people were shocked when they saw him; he was so disfigured that he hardly looked human.' And having finished with my thinking, I was still there unconscious of the time, unconcerned about the hundreds of other great works in that collection that I would not now even glimpse because of my time spent with Grunewald's Christ.

When finally I did leave the National Gallery, I brought with me a bought copy of this *Crucifixion*. It has been a valuable help in my prayer, although the colouring of Christ's body in it does not have the same quality as the original.

In fine weather you may prefer to meditate out of doors. Perhaps you are fortunate enough to have a quiet garden near at hand. If not, then you might have to regard outdoor meditation as a luxury to be enjoyed during holiday time or on a day off.

Even in winter it is no harm to dream of sun-drenched beaches, spectacular mountains or tranquil lake-sides — even a desert island — all as places suitable for meditation. Whether you are planning to meditate indoors or out of doors, the one essential requirement is that the place chosen should allow you enough freedom to become aware of what is happening inside you. Wherever you find yourself, you do carry within you a kind of psychological space, an alone-ness where the deepest 'you' lives.

EXERCISE 16: INNER SPACE

As we become accustomed to quietness and the practice of meditation, we will think of ourselves less and less in terms of body, social position, nationality, occupation, skills, knowledge, feelings or life-history. All these things are important, but they do not quite get to the heart of *who* I am. The real 'I' cannot be described in words, it can only be experienced in silence.

There is a great need to discover and be able to enter one's own inner space, for it is there most of all that one develops a true awareness of God. This space has been referred to by spiritual writers as 'the cave of the heart' and a 'nuptial chamber'. Symeon the New Theologian, a tenth century Greek monk, described it as 'the secret and intimate place in my spirit where I am embraced by the Lord'. The *Book of Psalms* (16.1 and 57.1) even speaks of God himself as being the place or space into which we can go for protection in times of distress: 'I trust in you for safety'; 'In the shadow of your wings I find protection'.

To discover and enter your inner space, sit comfortably and take yourself through the relaxation sequence outlined in the second half of exercise 14. With eyes closed, picture in front of your mind a square — any square whatever made out of any material whatever. Inside the square picture a circle, the circle being just a little smaller than the square and not touching it. Finally, inside the circle put 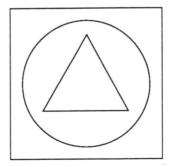 an equilateral triangle pointing upwards, the triangle being a little bit smaller than the circle and not touching

63

it. Let your mind rest on the figure of square containing circle containing triangle. Slowly begin to move towards the figure, observing how it grows larger as you approach. Notice how the square gets bigger and disappears out to the sides . . . the circle becoming a tunnel. Move into the tunnel and continue on towards the triangle . . . Pass through the centre of the triangle to the other side, and rest there . . .

EXERCISE 17: THE LORD'S SUPPER

Once within your inner space, you can use your imagination to reconstruct scenes from the gospel. This will require a little preparation beforehand, reading through gospel passages, selecting a scene for your meditation and taking notes (mental or written). It is probably best in the beginning to select just one favourite incident from the life of Jesus and meditate on that repeatedly, rather than go jumping from one part of the gospel to another. Remember that the more familiar you can become with the text and the more background knowledge you have, the more deeply you will be able to meditate. You may find it helpful, apart from reading the gospel text itself, to do other reading from books about the gospel or about Christ. As an example for this kind of exercise, the next paragraph gives notes for a meditation on the Lord's Supper (see *Matthew* 26.17-29; *Mark* 14.12-25 or *Luke* 22.7-38).

Beginning the meditation, check that you are sitting comfortably and (if you find it helpful) move to your inner space as described in exercise 16.

Next withdraw your five senses of seeing, hearing, taste, touch and smell from your actual physical surroundings and turn them inwards to the gospel scene.

Focus them on the place and people as described, and particularly on the person of Jesus.

Dim candle-light . . . dried mud floor of the upper room covered almost totally by roughly finished cushions and mats . . . a low table with wide flat loaves of unleavened bread and a large cup full of red wine. The feeding dish contains a whole lamb freshly roasted, for this is the evening of the Passover, to celebrate the night when God set us free from slavery to the Egyptians more than a thousand years ago.

The city has just about settled down after a hectic day's activity when Jesus takes his place at the head of the table and begins the customary ritual of prayers, readings, hymns and blessings that have accompanied the Paschal meal from time immemorial. . . . There is an uneasy silence as we reach out to the dish. The thrill of the Master's entry to the city a few days ago is now gone — there have been too many rumours — and we cannot forget those incredible utterances of Jesus concerning his own death. Will he be with us here to celebrate this time next year?

He is speaking: 'I have wanted so much to eat this Passover meal with you before I suffer! For I tell you, I will never eat it until it is given its full meaning in the Kingdom of God.' Bitter thoughts indeed for a Paschal celebration — and there is worse to come: 'I tell you that one of you will betray me — one who is eating with me.' Incredible! Who could it possibly be? — they blurt out, first one, then another and it is bedlam: 'It isn't me, that's for sure'; 'Master, you know that I would never . . .' And there's Peter, true to form: 'Lord, even if every one of these betrays you, I will die with you rather than betray you.' When the confusion has died down, Jesus repeats: 'It will be one of you twelve, one who dips his bread in the dish with me. The Son of Man will die as the Scriptures say he will; but how terrible for that man who betrays the Son of Man! It would have been better for that man if he had never been born!'

In stunned silence the meal drags on. It seems like ages before Jesus speaks again. And what's this he's doing? . . . handing us all pieces of bread and saying: 'Take and eat it, this is my body.' And now the cup . . . praying over it, passing it round, saying: 'Drink it, all of you, this is my blood, which seals God's covenant, my blood poured out for many for the forgiveness of sins.'

As you enter into this meditation, allow yourself to be struck by the physical details of the scene. One meditator told me that she was able to smell the roast lamb. Really *be* there, not as a spectator, but as someone involved.

Above all, allow your senses, your mind and your heart to be drawn to and filled with Jesus. When you have gone through the action and concluded with the final words of Jesus, spend at least a further ten minutes in silence.

Key 5: Sound

SOUND

I remember enjoying the feel of the sun on my face
that hot June afternoon as I pedalled my bicycle through
the Yeats Country in the West of Ireland. Returning after

a long absence, I realised I had forgotten just how
beautiful this countryside really is — particularly when
the sun shines. A few metres away from my quiet country
lane was the lake shore. I pulled my bike onto the grassy
bank and sat looking out across the gently rippling water.
The lake seemed to be inviting me to stillness. Lying
back, I pillowed my head on my pullover, my eyes closed
gently, and I became aware that my heart-beat and
breathing were slowing down after the exertion of my
cycling.

As I lazed sleepily, various little sounds of nature round about me floated into my consciousness — from the nearby trees the intermittent notes of a blackbird, the soft whirring sound of the breeze on the lake, and the steady dry rustling of leaves. I became steadily quieter within myself and, like the instruments in an orchestra, the sounds seemed to fall into different categories — birdsong, occasional distant moos from cows, barking of dogs and much closer, the baaing of a sheep, the little splashes at the lake's edge, and the continuous high buzz and drone of the insect world. Here, I thought, was a richness and depth of sound that no human orchestra could possibly match.

Then consciously I stopped thinking about orchestras and classes of sounds, and just allowed myself to surrender to the sound itself. No longer were there specific birds, insects, leaves or any other sources of sound. There was just a flowing, swirling tide, blending together into a vast symphony. And beyond the swarm of sounds that I could hear, I sensed there were infinitely more. In that moment I experienced a sense of completeness. I felt a great peace and knew a healing Presence, who was quietly and sweetly making some small adjustments somewhere deep inside me. The timeless Being that I sensed behind it all was — no, *is* kindly.

I felt loved.

And as I melted into the sounds, I seemed to hear echoing over and over again the words of an early Christian writer: 'Come to the Father — come to the Father. . . .' I felt at one with creation and somehow in touch with the ultimate Sound, the Word that speaks through the song of birds and the buzzing of insects.

We may not all have spectacular, unspoilt scenery like the Yeats Country on our door-steps. That does not mean we cannot enjoy meditation on the sounds of nature and even man-made sounds also. A favourite of my own is one that I like to call 'Concerto for bird and traffic orchestra'. I discovered it quite by accident in a local park.

EXERCISE 18: CONCERTO FOR BIRD AND TRAFFIC

For this meditation you may need to go to your nearest 'green belt' park, or it can be done in your garden, provided it is populated by at least one bird and is within hearing of some fairly distant traffic. The meditation may be done sitting comfortably (provided the weather is not cold or wet), standing or walking evenly up and down. Or you can even do it sitting indoors beside an open window.

Take a little time deciding on this and generally settling down, before turning your attention to the sounds round about you. At this point, unless you have decided to do a walking meditation, you may like to let your eyes close and begin the sound-meditation proper. Closing the eyes makes concentration on sound much easier.

Begin now to focus your attention on your hearing. Start by noting all the different sounds that you can hear — birds singing, dogs barking, children at play, men at work, aircraft, radio-cassettes, machinery and, of course, the traffic.

Do not let yourself be annoyed at some of the man-made sounds that you might usually object to, for instance, neighbours playing loud music in the garden next door. Stay nice and calm. Simply note each sound and then wait on the next, making no judgment for or against any one of them. Allow the sounds to happen and do not strain to hear them. Relax and let each sound register on your consciousness.

Gradually let your mind form a 'sound-picture', putting the sounds together in various groupings, for example: birds/animals . . . human voices . . . machines. Another way to group sounds might be: very near to me . . . some distance away . . . far away. Spend a little while letting the sounds flow through and around your mind. Enjoy this part of the exercise as much as possible. After about five minutes you should be ready for the core of the meditation.

From among all the sounds that are recurring, select the nearest and strongest of the bird noises. Preferably this will be of a song-bird such as a blackbird or thrush. However, even a crow will suffice, if need be! Study the pattern of the notes, pick out the melody, measure the silent interval before the melody is repeated. Let yourself be entertained for at least a few minutes by the bird-song.

Now turn your attention to the traffic noise. Just take note of the total *sound*. Wondering about what kind of vehicle might be causing each sound will only be a distraction. Observe the droning, ebb and flow pattern woven out of the hummings of many different engines. Hear it as a resonant base supporting the bird's solo performance. Note the contrast in pitch and rhythm between bird and traffic sounds. At this stage if you find your attention being drawn to other sounds such as the wind or the songs of other birds, then feel free to broaden the subject of your meditation to include these also. Spend a while reflecting on the different sounds and comparing them to one another.

71

Now begin to 'switch off' your mind and allow yourself to 'flow' with the sound that you are hearing. The important thing now is not the identity of the different sounds or where they are coming from, but simply the sensation of hearing.

Identify yourself completely with your sense of hearing — '*I am* hearing'. Let yourself *become* your hearing. Forget about yourself and simply *hear*. Whether you are hearing birds, animals, human or mechanical sounds doesn't matter now. What is important is the fact that you are listening, that you have been able to become physically and mentally passive to the sound that is reaching you. If you can manage to practise this kind of listening over a period of some weeks, you may be able to develop an awareness of that first 'Sound' that lies behind the countless millions of individual sounds that have ever vibrated throughout the world. For Christians the first Sound is associated with the eternal Word, the *Logos*, the Son of God, who appeared in the flesh as Jesus: 'Before the world was created, the Word already existed; he was with God, and he was the same as God' (*John* 1.1), and 'The Word became a human being and, full of grace and truth, lived among us' (*John* 1.14). We may say that God is Sound almost in the same way as we say that God is Love. Just as it is possible to come to know God through the experience of human love, so also it is possible to be brought to a sense of God through the rich texture of sound that fills the universe. We can be relaxed and brought to wholeness by listening to the pure sounds of nature or the music of great composers or by the repetition of a simple chant or mantra. There is absolutely no sound, however jarring it may seem at first, that we cannot use in order to get closer to God in a listening meditation. Nevertheless, we will find that meditating through certain natural or musical sounds is easier and more effective than through others. My own choice of music for meditation ranges from the majestic, subtle choral work of Bach's *Mass in B Minor* to some repetitive Sanskrit chants from Fr Bede Griffith's ashram in South India.

EXERCISE 19: MEDITATION THROUGH MUSIC

Your cassette, record or CD player can be an invaluable help to meditation — but only if you are prepared to give all your attention to the music and not treat it as mere background! Give some thought to choosing the correct piece, whether instrumental, vocal, classical, sacred, folk or whatever. There are no hard and fast rules here. Dance music or the foot-tapping, hand-clapping variety can be useful for getting rid of nervous energy, but must be followed up by at least ten minutes of stillness if it is to be of real benefit. Tranquil instrumental or religious music can bring you more immediately into meditative silence.

Begin by selecting a piece of music that is not too long, that you reckon is good for you and that you look forward to hearing. Set it up so that it is ready to play.

Find a comfortable sitting position, making sure that your back is fairly straight, and take some time to relax your body and mind. You may like to use the technique given in the last chapter (exercise 14), to help you to do this.

Focus on your sense of hearing. First notice any sounds within the room, then within the house, and finally outside.

Now turn your attention in anticipation to the music

you are about to hear. Calmly switch on your player and listen.

In the beginning think about what you are hearing. Identify different instruments and voices. See how they relate to one another. Study the pattern of harmony and melody and the different tones. You may even like to form a 'picture' of the music in your mind. In other words, at this stage of your meditation, your mind is actively exploring what your ears are taking in. You are mentally alert. At some point you will feel that you have completed your examination of the musical details. You may now begin to ease back your thinking. Allow your mind to slow down. Let yourself enjoy the music.  Because of your earlier preparation what will be happening now is that you will become absorbed in the music and yet totally relaxed. Remain this way if you can, until the piece is concluded, and then stay in silence for at least another ten minutes.

You will have seen that in this type of meditation there is a 'thinking' stage followed by a 'mental relaxation' stage. It is the latter, sometimes called 'contemplation', that is the heart of the exercise. It will be done more successfully, the more thoroughly you have prepared for the 'thinking' stage. For example, you might find out what you can about the composer of the music, the circumstances under which it was written and so on. You may want to study the complete score and in the case of vocal music, make sure you know all the words beforehand. This kind of detail is not strictly necessary for meditation, of course, but you will find that some

such preparation will help you avoid much and perhaps
all mental distraction when you start to contemplate.
Exerting your mind in the first part of the meditation
will make it more inclined to rest, be still and therefore,
not subject to distraction in the second part.

Sound Meditations Check-List

1. Select your sound – natural, man-made,

   musical

2. Posture, relax limbs, become aware of

   your breathing. . . hearing

3. Explore the sound with your mind

4. Relax your mind – be still

EXERCISE 20: MANTRA RECITATION

Repetitive chanting has been widely used from the
earliest times to make oneself present to God. Mantra
chanting and recitation are practised universally by
Hindus and Buddhists in Asia, and are becoming fairly
common also in the west. Up to the 1960s the Roman
Catholic Church used litany responses in Latin which
were sung over and over again to beautiful Gregorian
melodies. The religious practice of Christians in many
parts of the world has always found space for the simple
prayer of few words, spoken or sung repetitively. Recently
I visited an old people's home in rural Ireland. I was
touched by the prayer of one old lady, apparently senile,
who was seated in a wheel-chair. During the entire time I
was in the ward, she intoned the words: 'Jesus, Jesus,

come to me.' Half-spoken, half-sung, the droning rhythm of these words formed a back-ground to the conversation I was having with the patient I had come to visit. The old woman cannot have been fully conscious of the meaning of her words — but then, who of us can say that he/she is *fully* conscious of what our words mean? Besides, the power of this kind of prayer does not depend entirely on understanding. It has a lot also to do with faith and with the sound that is made. Very often people are more deeply moved by a chanted Latin or Sanskrit phrase whose meaning they do not understand, than they are by an equivalent phrase in their own everyday language. Perhaps it is because some languages are more musical than others, or because a novel exotic sound draws us more quickly to a new kind of awareness. It has less association with familiar words and ideas that might easily distract us in our prayer.

To start on this simplest form of meditation, you will need to select a suitable mantra. This should harmonise with what you believe in your inmost heart. By its very nature your mantra is designed to bring about an intimacy between you and God.

For a Christian there is a wide variety of mantras to pick from, for example: 'Jesus, Son of the living God, have mercy on me a sinner.' This is the 'Jesus prayer' and has been used by Christian monks as far back as the second century.

The short phrases from the bible given in chapter two can all be used for mantra recitation.

A very ancient mantra, whose use is being revived in recent times by Benedictine monks, is *Maranatha.* This is Aramaic, the language spoken in the Holy Land at the time of Jesus. It is in fact two words, either *Marana tha* (Our Lord come!) or *Maran Atha* (the Lord has come). The ambiguity of meaning takes nothing from its effec-

76

tiveness and may indeed help us in making the transition from the 'thinking' stage to the 'contemplation' stage in meditation (see exercise 19).

Having decided what mantra you are going to use, begin as usual by making yourself comfortable in any sitting position. Make sure that your back is fairly straight. Check that the different areas of your body are relaxed, and are so positioned that they can relax: your left leg . . . right leg . . . back. . . left arm. . . right arm . . . head and neck. As you go through this sequence, gently move each limb to where it is most comfortable. Let your eyes close. Become aware of your breathing — do not attempt to control its speed. Stay with the rhythm of the breath for a while. Now gently begin to think about your mantra. Repeat it mentally, keeping time with your breathing, should you find this helpful. If you have difficulty getting in touch with your breathing, you may simply repeat the mantra in your mind either fast or slowly, depending on which is easier for you. Keep up the repetition of your mantra for the entire duration of your meditation.

You will not be meditating for long, when you will discover that you have been distracted from your mantra, and that you have stopped repeating it in your mind. When this happens, quietly bring your attention back to the mantra and begin reciting it again. You will find yourself having to do this many times. Do not be disappointed with yourself for being distracted. Above all, do not think that your meditation has 'failed' because of distraction. Meditation is like a journey, but a journey that we are always beginning again and again. Success does not consist in beautiful experiences or a sense of relaxation or inner peace. Indeed, one should hardly speak of success at all in the context of meditation. What counts is not 'success', but being faithful. So whatever may be happening or not happening in your meditation, resolve to keep up your practice no matter what. As you devote your time, your attention and your heart to God, he will be slowly and gently moulding you — spirit, mind, emotions, senses and even your body — into that person that he in his love created you to be.

Finally, here is a meditation exercise that combines mantra recitation with the kind of gospel meditation outlined in chapter 4 (exercise 17).

EXERCISE 21: THE BLIND MAN

The gospel scene in this meditation is *Mark* 10.46 -52, which describes how Jesus healed the beggar Bartimaeus of his blindness. By 'experiencing' through meditation something of what it is like to be physically blind, we can with God's help come to know our own real spiritual blindness.

As in the earlier meditations of this chapter, sit comfortably, keeping your back upright. Become aware of your breathing for two or three minutes. Now think of the mantra which was the blind man's plea: 'Jesus, Son of David! Take pity on me!' Match or mould the words 'Jesus, Son of David' to your inhalation; and the words 'take pity on me' to your exhalation. Remember to match words to breath and not breath to words. When you have the words and your breathing moving comfortably together, relax for a few moments.

Turning now to the scene from *Mark* 10.46 -52, close your eyes and turn your senses of seeing, hearing, taste, touch and smell inwards. 'Hear', 'touch' and 'smell' within your imagination, what Bartimaeus must have heard, touched and smelt that day. The following notes may help you through this part of the meditation.

78

What a life! Sitting here in the dust and heat . . . How much will it be today? Can hardly be worse than yesterday — six miserable drachmas, and half of this to Levi and his gang of parasites for the privilege of this spot.

It's the best part of the road, just outside the Jerusalem Gate. You can catch all the pilgrims on their way up to the Temple in Jerusalem.

Privilege indeed! How they blather about the Lord and his wonderful deeds — and alms-giving! The few who give you anything really make you feel it — the airs they think I do not sense because of my blindness . . . This is no life for anyone. If only I could see.

I can hear them now — the first of the many groups that will pass today . . . Sounds like a fair crowd this early in the day — yes, a really big crowd. They should be worth a few drachmas.

They seem to be excited about something — everybody talking at once. They won't even notice me.

'Hello there, alms for the blind! Alms for the love of God!'

'Quiet, beggar! Jesus of Nazareth is passing.'

Jesus of Nazareth! Can it be possible? The one they say is the Messiah, the Son of the great King David? Perhaps . . . perhaps he can cure me! I've got nothing to lose. 'Jesus! Jesus, Son of David! take pity on me!'

'Will you be quiet?'

'I will not! — Jesus, Son of David, take pity on me!'

From this point on, bring your attention back to your breathing and continue to repeat those words: 'Jesus, Son of David! Take pity on me!' to the rhythm of your breathing for at least a further ten minutes.

You may if you like preface this meditation with exercise 16: *Inner Space* from the last chapter. It may make it easier for you focus your senses and feelings within the gospel scene. Also, please note the remarks on page 64 about preparing gospel meditations.

Key 6: Rhythm

RHYTHM

Getting in touch with the rhythms of nature and of your body is what this chapter is about. Each of the exercises that follow begins with relaxation and stillness in order that you can tune in to these rhythms. The first three exercises will help you get in touch with your heart-beat.

EXERCISE 22: HEART MONITOR

Lying Down: Wearing loose comfortable clothing, lie down on the carpeted floor of your room. Have your feet eight to twelve inches apart, arms by your side a little bit away from your body and check that you are lying in a straight line. Draw your toes up towards your body and your heels away from your body in a stretching movement and relax. Gently roll your head from side to side, taking stiffness out of your neck and finish with your head in a position where it can rest comfortably. Relax, allow your eyes to close and focus all your attention on your body. 'Listen' firstly to the rhythm of your breathing — then to the rhythm of your heart-beat.

If you have difficulty detecting either of these body-rhythms, this may be because — due to your relaxed state — your breathing may be very quiet and your heart-beat very gentle. You may like to do a little floor-level limbering-up which will cause both the heart and the lungs to work a bit harder. Raise your right leg just clear of the floor (a few inches will be enough). Holding the foot steady, move your toes backwards and forwards a number of times, all the while being aware of how your toe-joints are being loosened up. Now, holding the leg straight, work your foot backwards and forwards, again keeping your attention where the stretching, loosening action is taking place — this time in your ankle. Next, rotate your foot in one direction for a few rounds, and then in the other direction. Shift your attention from your ankle to your knee next as you alternately bend and straighten your leg at the knee. And, as with the ankle, move on then to a rotating movement of your lower leg around your knee — first in one direction, then in the other. Straightening out the entire leg, move it up into the vertical, then down almost to the floor and then up and down a few more times. This loosening of the hip and groin can be continued by going on to a rotating movement of the entire leg, first in one, then in the other direction. Finally, lower your leg slowly to the ground and relax completely.

Should the above routine be too strenuous for you, you may perform just as much of it as is suitable for you, omit the remainder, and then relax as above. As you lie there in the few minutes after the exertion, you will certainly be aware of your rapid breathing. Your heart-beat too will have been speeded up and may even be thumping a little under the left side of your rib cage. You may like to bring your right hand across and place it on the left side of your chest, just beneath the breast and with your fingers feel for the heart-beat. When you are satisfied that you have located it, bring your arm back to your right side again, and stay in contact with the vibrating sensation in your chest. 'Listen' attentively for some time to this vital movement.

Take note of the speed at which your heart is beating, and in particular of how it slows down gradually as you relax. Be aware of exactly where its beating, vibrating motion is located. Do you get any sense of an expanding-contracting movement? Can you find any pattern in the heart-beat? Do you find this beating movement reassuring and comforting, or do you find it distressing in any way? On the basis of your body awareness of the heart's beating, you may like to imagine what it might look like. Forget about the operating room sequences you may have seen on television, or anything you may have learned in anatomy and physiology. Just form an image that is based solely on what you are aware is going on at this moment in your body. This dynamic image can serve as your own personal heart monitor. You will be able to return to it any time you like to spot-check the way your heart is running. It will give you an early warning should your heart be coming under strain due to physical exertion, or psychological or social pressure. This will allow you to take corrective action early on, thus protecting your heart. But there is more to it than this. A heart that is coming under strain is saying something important to its owner. Perhaps he/she is working too hard? Maybe he/she is being too confrontative with people? Perhaps he/she needs to lose weight or spend more time out of doors, or take a holiday? Or perhaps he/she is over-exercising?

Exercising: The next time you go jogging, or put on a 'shape-tape', or mow the lawn, or carry the bin out — before you start at all, get in touch with your heart-beat. Make sure that its movement is easy and gentle, almost undetectable. If, at the beginning of manual work, or at any time during it, you find that your heart is racing — then do not continue. Relax completely, if possible lying on your back. Allow your heart-beat to slow down. It might be telling you to lighten your level of physical exertion, at least for the moment. Pay heed to it!

EXERCISE 23: LIVING HEART

Lying down, spend some time being aware of your heart-beat. Take note of as many details as you can: speed, strength, location, *etc.* Form a visual image of its movement. Pay attention to any other sensations that may be there in the region of your heart. Remind yourself that your heart has been beating non-stop from the time you were in your mother's womb, and will remain beating right through your bodily life. You do not have to decide to make it beat — it continues on, through your waking and sleeping, whether you are aware of it or not. Because it beats, you are alive now, at this moment. Yet, though your living, beating heart is given to you as a gift, or indeed as *the* gift of life, you nonetheless are able to influence it in a number of ways. Your activity and your rest make it beat fast or slow. Congenital defects apart, the pattern of its rhythm can be affected for better or worse by your temperament, the things you eat and drink, and your life-style. Of course, the state of your heart, as mentioned above, fundamentally depends on the constitution you had when you were born, Nevertheless, if you started off your life with a sound, healthy heart, then the way it is now and in the future will broadly reflect the way you live — your philosophy of life, your values, your occupation, relationships, interests and hopes. No part of your body is more fully *you* than your heart. Listen to it, reflecting on some of the points mentioned above, and it will teach you many things.

EXERCISE 24: HEART MANTRA

Again lie on your back, listening to and reflecting on your heart-beat. As you study the beat closely, you will notice that it has a kind of 'one-two-one-two' rhythmic pattern. Now imagine that the 'one-beat' is sounding the syllable *Jes-* while the 'two-beat' is sounding *-us*. It will be as if each 'one-two' of your heart-beat is speaking the word *Jes-us* as a kind of mantra. Stay with the 'Jesus' mantra for some time, moulding the word to your heart-beat. Make it a habit that, every time you become aware of your heart's beating, you will 'hear' it repeating the holy name 'Jesus'. In time you will not even need to associate the mantra with the heart-pulse consciously. Your heart will itself beat out the name of Jesus. You will then be praying, not with your lips or your mind, but quite literally with your heart. Furthermore, you will be able to pray when your conscious mind is on other things and even when you are asleep. The words of Saint Paul: 'Pray at all times' (I *Thessalonians* 5.17) refers to prayer of this kind, rather than using word-prayers or trying to hold God in our consciousness all the time — an impossible undertaking. Using your heart mantra will help you build up an attitude of prayer that can be effective twenty-four hours of the day. Each time you practise it, you will deepen to some extent your heart's attitude towards God.

Apart from the rhythms of our bodies, such as the heart-beat and the breath, there are also rhythms in the natural world round about us with which we can get in tune.

In fact, we tend automatically to respond to the main cycles of nature. We sleep at night-time and are awake during the day. A day of rest or Sabbath for every six days of work or activity, corresponds to a deep physiological and psychological need. The changing seasons of the year draw us with them: winter stimulating us to burn off excess energy, summer inviting us to a gentler out of door tempo. The cycle of growth and decay which we witness in plant life reminds us that there are seasons in our lives too: childhood, adolescence, maturity and old age. There is 'the time for birth and the time for death, the time for planting and the time for pulling up' (*Ecclesiastes* 3.2). Whether it is a question of working, eating,  socialising, engaging in sports or travelling; our nature is to set up patterns of activity and rest based on the hours of the day, the days of the week or month, and the seasons both of the year and of our life-span itself. These patterns hold for religion too, as shown by Sunday worship and the way the major Christian fesivals of Christmas and Easter are situated respectively in mid-winter and at the end of spring. And there are rituals associated with family life, birth, initiation into adult life, sickness and death (seen as an entry into a new life).

Being sensitive to the rhythms of nature helps to keep us sane and healthy. One need only reflect on the strain produced by prolonged night-shift working or by widely-varying meal times, to see this — while recognising that many people's job situations give them little choice in these matters. Allowing our life to flow with, rather than against, the pulse of nature relieves us of stress and saves energy. In the beginning it takes a little effort and some self-discipline to establish good habits like eating when possible at a fixed time or taking a regular day off. In a short time the practice becomes almost effortless and our greater sense of wholeness makes it easier to face the challenges of daily living.

The next two exercises are related to the rhythm of day/night.

TUNING IN TO NATURE

1. Be *still* in body and mind

2. Become *aware* of any one natural rhythm

3. *Stay with* that rhythm for a while

4. Relax and 'flow' with the rhythm

5. *Receive* nature's energy

EXERCISE 25: DAWN MEDITATION

Doing this meditation requires getting up a little before sunrise. For most people spring and autumn are the most practical times of year for this. During summer the sun rises really early. During winter it rises so late that your work demands or the rest of the family are likely to stampede into your life before you can complete the meditation. Finish your morning toilet and then do some gentle physical exercise such as a short walk or a few yoga postures near an open window.

Lie down and make yourself comfortable, or sit (with your light switched off) facing the window if possible. Perhaps you will already be able to pick up the first sounds of an awakening world: a bird chirping, a dog barking or a distant car starting up? Slowly begin to move — stretching, loosening up, coming to life. Be fully conscious of each move that you make. Realise that you are not just an individual starting his day, but part of some great release of fresh energy. Light and life are coming into the world to millions of living creatures and people and to you. As you now begin to move more energetically, gratefully receive what is being offered to you from God as part of his creation. As the world brightens, face eastwards and open your eyes to the new light of day. See yourself as being one with all living beings that are beginning this new day. When you have finished exercising, spend some time in silence. Relax your body and your mind and allow the sounds, the light and the warmth of the morning to nourish you. This whole sequence could last a half-hour or more.

If you would like to develop your experimental early rising into a habit, there are several ways in which you can enrich your dawn meditation. The bible begins with the account of creation described in the first two chapters of the *Book of Genesis*. These chapters can lend substance to your reflections. As you lie in the dark on the floor of your room, and before you start moving, ponder the words: 'In the beginning, when God created the universe. . . everything was engulfed in total darkness' (*Genesis* 1.1-2). As you begin to hear the sounds of nature, reflect on: 'God created . . . all kinds of birds. And God was pleased with what he saw' (*Genesis* 1.21). As you first become aware of dawning light, you might contemplate: 'Then God commanded, "Let there be light" — and light appeared. God was pleased with what he saw. Then he separated the light from the darkness, and he named the light "Day" and the darkness "Night" ' (*Genesis* 1.3-5).

The beginning of Saint John's Gospel takes up the same themes. You may like to use it instead of *Genesis,* especially lines like: 'Through him God made all things; not one thing in all creation was made without him. The Word was the source of life, and this life brought light to mankind. The light shines in the darkness, and the darkness has never put it out' (*John* 1.3-5); 'This was the real light — the light that comes into the world and shines on all mankind' (*John* 1.9).

Whenever you are blessed with the opportunity of silently witnessing the sun's rising, why not make that the focus of your meditation? Provided it is not too cold for you, the ideal would be to sit or stand facing the rising sun, reflecting on the gospel words: 'Our God is merciful and tender. He will cause the bright dawn of salvation to rise on us and to shine from heaven on all those who live in the dark shadow of death, to guide our steps into the path of peace' (*Luke* 1.78-79).

EXERCISE 26: SUNSET MEDITATION

Sunset or nightfall has always been a special time for prayer in Christianity and indeed in all the world religions. This prayer balances the prayer of morning. We are invited to slow down, to rest, to become still and at the same time, attentive to God. Whenever you have the opportunity — probably in your holiday time — sit or stand in silence, facing the setting sun. This is particularly beautiful when it is watched slowly sinking into the western sea. If you like, use a line of Scripture to help you meditate, for example *Psalm* 113.3 or *Ephesians* 4.26: 'From the rising of the sun to its setting, may the name of the Lord be praised!'; and 'the sun must not be allowed to go down, while you are still angry'.

If the weather is cold or wet and you are unable to see the sun — then, as it begins to get dark, sit near the window of your bedroom, with the curtains open, You might like to set up a crucifix or an ikon with a candle, night-lights, incense, etc. As you begin, you will scarcely notice the light of the candle — your attention will be drawn by the day-light coming in from outside. Take a little time to make sure that you are in a comfortable, steady position. Look ahead of you and take note of what you can see in the light of day: the furnishings of your room, the window frame and everything that you can see outside — trees, walls, poles, buildings, etc. Do not strain to see. Just relax and allow objects to impinge on your consciousness.

Next, slowly close your eyes and listen to the sounds of evening. Pay particular attention to the sounds of nature, but include also man-made sounds such as traffic, stereos and, of course, the human voice. From this point on open or close your eyes at will. Become aware of the pulsating stream of life behind all that you can see and hear. With the passing of time, keep in touch with any changes that are taking place — the sky turning a deeper blue, birds becoming silent, house and street lights coming on, and so forth. Notice how your candle light now appears brighter and your religious image becomes more 'alive'. Become conscious of what is happening within you — your breath, heart-beat and your whole body slowing down and becoming more relaxed. Deliberately allow yourself to go with the movement of nature — from the exertion and speed of day to the rest and stillness of night. The words of *Psalm* 104.23 beautifully capture the mood of this time of day: 'People go out to do their work and keep working until evening'; 'The sun knows the time to set. You make the darkness, and it is night' (verses 19-20).

As the darkness takes over more and more, relax your mind completely. Do not consciously see or hear. Be content to be part of the Creator's plan. And (assuming that you do not have pressing responsibilities) what he is inviting you to at this time of day is rest, refreshment of body and spirit. Remain on in silence for as long as you wish. Then gently become aware of your surroundings, slowly open your eyes and let them be drawn to your ikon or crucifix lit up by the candle. Again spend a little time in silence before bringing your meditation to an end.

Key 7: Simplicity

SIMPLICITY

'Your are what you eat'; yet we do not give enough thought to the question of what we eat. We eat almost unconsciously, out of habit. We eat too much or too little. Our diets are often poorly balanced and the market for 'junk' foods con-  tinues to expand. How many times we are tempted by the best prepared food and over- eat — paying for it later in discomfort and disrupted work schedules. I can say that I really enjoyed a birthday cele- bration gin and tonic with my friends, and the sumptuous lunch of lasagna, rich in prime minced steak, washed down with two glasses of Liebfraumilch, followed by nutty plum pudding and brandy butter, with a cup of coffee. Later, when I found it hard to concentrate on my work and had my stomach competing for attention with a person who had come to me looking for guidance, I knew that I had overdone it. And my meditation that evening was beset with distractions.

What we eat and drink greatly affects our work and our prayer. If we are serious about meditation, we will have to resolve to eat and live simply and intelligently. There are a few general rules in regard to balancing foods that give energy and heat with those that provide roughage and help cleanse the system. But then, different foods suit different people. How much should I eat, and when? Should my main meal be at midday or in the evening? What about special diets, fasting and vegetarianism? The answers to these questions are to be found only inside yourself. There are easy awareness exercises that can put you in touch with what food, drink and intoxicants do for you or to you. By 'listening' to your body you can learn which foods and how much are good, and which are bad for you personally.

One of the things that I myself learnt from listening to my digestive system was that I should give up eating meat. It wasn't that meat-eating was damaging my health in any obvious way. It was simply that I was becoming more and more aware that eating pork, beef and mutton left me with a heavy, slightly unpleasant feeling in my stomach that lasted for several hours. For me meat, while tempting, is not easily digested. That had been the case for most of my life. And yet, it was not until I tried 'sensing' what was going on inside me that I really became conscious of the fact and was able to do something about it. Over a period of about two years, I gradually reduced my meat intake, and eventually gave it up entirely.

If you are interested in sensing what your last meal is doing in your digestive system right now, then try the following exercise.

EXERCISE 27: STOMACH AWARENESS

Sit quietly for a few moments with your eyes closed. Bring your awareness to the region of your stomach and digestive tract, i.e., from just below the rib cage to about three inches below the navel. If you have eaten recently, the digestive process is in full spate, breaking your food down into life-giving nutrients and waste products. First of all, you will notice (and may have been only too well aware of it before you began this exercise) any uncomfortable feeling. Locate the precise points where there is discomfort, heaviness, a sense of being overfull, or any other feeling of unease. Stay with these feelings themselves — experiencing them, rather than thinking about them — for a little while.

Next move on to the question: why is it there? Most of the time, the answer to this question is to be found in what you have eaten and drunk in the past number of hours. Think in turn about the different food items that made up your last meal. Relate each of them to what you are feeling in your  stomach now. Put together a short-list of 'suspects'. Bear in mind too that your present perhaps uneasy stomach may be the result not of the kinds of things you have eaten, but rather the amount, or the speed at which you ate, or the fact that you were physically or emotionally tense when you were at table. When we are tense we sometimes eat mouthfuls of air between bites. Finish off by making some resolution concerning your future eating habits.

The above type of reflection can also, of course, be usefully carried out when your digestion is feeling fine.

Sometime when you are eating alone, try taking a mouthful and eating slowly. Keep your awareness focused as you chew and swallow. Follow the food as it makes its way downwards. Be conscious of it as it (temporarily) comes to rest in your stomach.

EXERCISE 28: WATER DRINKING

The next time you are really thirsty, drink a glass of cool water slowly and with full awareness. This is best done on an empty stomach. Follow the water as it passes through your mouth and the inside of your cheeks. Stay with it on its way down your throat. Notice how, on reaching the bottom of the rib cage, it feels as though it were dividing up into little streams. A little further down these 'streams' seem to sub-divide further, becoming smaller until they are completely absorbed.

As you develop the practice of eating and drinking deliberately, your awareness of what food and drink is doing to your insides will become more and more refined. You will find yourself moving gradually to a healthier eating pattern, one that is shaped by your body's real need for nutrition and digestibility, rather than taste alone. And in this matter, what your stomach can sense is a much more reliable guide than what your palate desires. You will tend to seek out certain foods (raw fruits, vegetables) as light, quickly assimilated and refreshing; others (whole grains, nuts, pulses) as more substantial body-builders and energy-givers. You may find, as I did, that red meat, while full of energy, exacts its toll in terms of digestion. When you find that your stomach is still working hard, five hours later, on that steak you had for lunch, then it is certainly time to cut back. Junk foods will reveal their true character to your digestive system, if not to your taste, when you have a 'full but dead' kind of feeling, that might equally well have been produced by a diet of cotton wool or cardboard. In any case, while you can learn much about healthy eating from diet sheets, let your own self-awareness be the ultimate judge of what is suitable for you, and when, and how much. And do not be afraid of skipping a meal occasionally, when you just don't feel like eating. It may simply be your stomach telling you that it needs a rest.

Body awareness exercises can also help us become conscious of our addictions. Everyone know about the obvious ones; like drug and tobacco dependency, alcoholism and compulsive gambling. But what about our quantities of strong coffee or tea, taken to 'get us through the day'; or, on the other hand, the tablet without which 'I'll never sleep at all'. Of course there are times in our lives when medication is prescribed and needed. Yet it is good to take note as to whether we are not perhaps a little 'hooked' on some item or other — something we feel we cannot do without, and yet may be acting as a disguise for something else within. Comfort-eating tells its own story, but it is not an easy story to hear within oneself. What am I hungry for, that I try to fill that gap with chocolate and cream eclairs? All these are substitutes for a real experience of inner peace and joy. If I have not been opened up to the happiness which is God's gift, then I must of necessity seek my happiness in other ways. Speaking with the woman at the well, Jesus compared the life he is offering to water:'Whoever drinks the water that I will give him will never be thirsty again. The water that I will give him will become in him a spring which will provide him with life-giving water and give him eternal life' (*John* 4.14). Meditation is about tuning in to this 'living water' and, at the same time, letting go of phoney pleasures. It can help us grow free bit by bit from our addictions.

If you are taking some form of sedation, it may be difficult to focus yourself sufficiently to follow through with an extended awareness exercise. However, you might just sit quietly from time to time and monitor your body feelings. How am I feeling all round? What sensations do I have in my head? . . . stomach? . . . chest? How is my heart-beat? . . . my breathing?

EXERCISE 29: DETACHMENT

This meditation is inspired by a line from the Prophet *Jeremiah* (29.13): 'You will seek me, and you will find me because you will seek me with all your heart.'

Sit comfortably anywhere in your home, and relax. Spend some time thinking about all the things you own in the world — money, clothes, furnishings, mod-cons, luxury hi-fi and stereo, perhaps even this house. As you sit there in the room, imagine that a furniture van is pulling up in the street just outside. Soon after, the front door opens and two removal men come in. In your imagination see them as they calmly set to the task of loading the contents of the house into their van.

Pay attention to each item as it is removed: bed, table, chairs, carpets, TV, stereo, curtains, kitchen utensils, electrical appliances, etc. What are your feelings as they place your cash, cheque-book, bank pass, visa and access cards, jewellery, photographs, letters and other personal belongings in a case and leave? The house is now totally emptied, and you are about to leave it behind too, taking with you only what you can carry.

As your car is also gone, you walk away, saying good-bye to all the people that you love most: spouse, children, parents, family, close friends. You are going to a distant country and will not be seeing them again. Understand that when you have gone, you will be forgotten, even by those who loved and respected you most . . .

As you become conscious of your aloneness, without friends and owning nothing; think about what is still left to you — your talents, your ability to work, to think and to love . . . your strength and health . . . your senses of seeing, hearing, touch, taste  and smell . . . One by one, imagine yourself deprived of each one of these.

You are now left with nothing but God alone. In your poverty focus on him. If it helps, picture some ikon of the Lord, or repeat a mantra. Try to seek him 'with all your heart.' You may at this point like to speak to him from your heart, using other lines of Scripture, e.g.: 'You are my Lord; you are everything that I have.' (*Psalm* 16.2); 'O God, you are my God, and I long for you. My whole being desires you' (*Psalm* 63.1); 'Listen to me, Lord, and answer me, for I am helpless and weak' (*Psalm* 86.1). You are now at the core of the meditation, so spend some time alone with the Lord in silence. At the end of that time, become aware of your feelings. Do you have any sense of having been cleansed or set free? Are you at peace in your emptiness? Any sense of being close to a loving God?

Begin now to reverse the process of separating yourself from people and things. As in a film which is slowly run backwards, receive back one by one your talents and gifts of mind and body, your loved ones and your possessions. As you welcome each one back, accept it with gratitude as a present from God. Hold it in your heart, appreciating fully just how much it means to you. When finally everything is as it was, ponder God's greatness and love, reflecting on the words: 'I was born with nothing, and I will die with nothing. The Lord gave, and now he has taken away. May his name be praised' (*Job* 1.21).

This kind of meditation will help you to 'count your blessings', but also to overcome greed and possessiveness. As you realise that your real wealth comes as a gift from God, you will become more free of the powerful attraction of money and what money can buy. You will be drawn to simplicity and quietness and will understand that (in the words of Saint Augustine) 'it is better to need little than to have much'. For example, you may find yourself more often choosing to walk rather than take the car for short journeys. The exercise is good, but more than that, you will be consuming less, polluting the atmosphere less and even enjoying the solitude which the simple act of walking gives you.

By living more simply you will be taking your first tiny step towards looking at some of the most serious problems threatening the world today. Third world hunger, industrial pollution, the destruction of forests and the earth's atmosphere, and injustice of every kind are taking place mainly because too many of us are consuming too much and wanting too much. By reflecting on and becoming aware of what you eat, drink, use, waste or consume in any way, you may be starting a revolution. You may reach the conclusion that you can live happily on only a fraction of the goods and services that advertisers try to convince us are necessary. You will be leaving more of the world's resources for others — hopefully those who need them most.

The next exercise is designed to help you assess what you really need in order to live simply but happily.

EXERCISE 30: REFLECTION ON LIFE–STYLE

Begin by listing the things that you consider absolutely necessary for you personally (do not include the needs of your family members at this stage). Use your imagination freely as you do this. You might picture yourself starting up life in a different city or in the remote countryside. Make a list of the bare essentials that you will need from the very first day, in terms of shelter, clothing and food. Write each item down on a piece of paper. As you write it down, see yourself as you make use of it. When you are satisfied that your list is complete, go through it again and in regard to everything that is on it, ask yourself the question: 'Could I survive without this?' See if you can *reduce* your list of essentials in this way. Encourage yourself with the thought that you are identifying in some way with the simple way of life that Jesus lived: 'Foxes have holes, and birds have nests, but the Son of Man has nowhere to lie down and rest' (*Matthew* 8.20).

Next, add to the list just those things and services that would enhance the quality of your living, without taking away your peace. Carefully reflect on each one, trying to see how it might be genuinely beneficial in terms of health . . . prayer . . . love and service of others. If it does not check out under one or other of these headings, do not put it on your list. Go on to include the needs of your family or any other persons in your care. Again cater for their needs rather than their wants, though obviously in the real situation you would have to negotiate with them in regard to whether something was a 'need' or a 'want'.

When you have completed the above lists of needs, you might like to make a personal or a family budget. How much do you, and your family, need to live on.

Compare that with what you are actually living on. Look for ways to economise.

WHO AM I?

I am not . . .

1. My possessions

2. What others think of me

3. My body and my senses

4. My mind and my heart

EXERCISE 31: THE TEMPTATIONS OF JESUS

The practice of fasting has from time immemorial been associated with prayer and meditation in all the world's religions. The reason is probably that our body's hunger or thirst can remind us of our deep need for God, as expressed in *Psalm* 42.1: 'As a deer longs for a stream of cool water, so I long for you, O God.' Jesus himself set us an example by his forty days fasting in the wilderness.

The temptations that he was subjected to during that time are the theme of this meditation, which is based on *Matthew* 4.1-11 and *Luke* 4.1-12.

You can prepare yourself for this meditation by carefully reading these gospel passages, by sitting still, going into your 'inner space' and turning your five senses inwards (see exercises 14, 16 and 17). If you like, you can make use of the following notes to help you construct the scene in your imagination:

Dawning sun-light touches the east cliff-face. Thank God for the sun — the desert night chills you to the bone when you've already been without food for thirty-two days — funny how the heat of the day, even out of the shade, seems to affect you less as time goes on. It just makes it harder to concentrate on anything — and I really need concentration right now. I leave my shallow cave and go up the cleft a little — my seat for the day, a smooth stone positioned to catch the dawning warming sunlight, but also close enough to the cliff overhang so as to give shade from the scorching heat of midday.

The thoughts of yesterday and the day before regain their sinister fascination as the day warms . . . Why this desert, this gnawing hunger, the heat, the cold, the tiredness? There is bread — the best of food and drink, comforts and even the service of angels for the Son of Man, to be had at any time for the wishing. Why go on this way? What are you trying to prove? . . . My brothers and sisters have to go without, and I will be exactly as they are . . . 'But they are not worth it — eat your bread instead!'. . . Scripture says: 'Man cannot live on bread alone, but needs every word that God speaks.'

I am hungry and, worse still, the hot breeze from the sands is insufficient to keep away the tiny flies that torment my eyes, nose and ears. It is the time of day when the heat and discomfort are at their worst . . . Fear closes in — fear of the hurt and pain of my last three years on earth, and of the hours of darkness that lie at the end. Again the tempting possibility comes to mind with unusual persuasion . . . 'Give up — you don't have to suffer anything. Don't let yourself get hurt — for

Scripture says: 'God will give orders to his angels about you; they will hold you up with their hands, so that not even your feet will be hurt on the stones' . . . No! I will carry on. It is the Father's will, and Scripture also says: 'Do not put the Lord your God to the test.'

The Tempter is closer than ever . . . 'Jesus, you cannot win. Even if you are mad enough to die for them, they will still not listen. Don't you know what they are like, too stupid to understand your kind of love? . . . Now if you really want to be master of this world: of Jerusalem, Rome, Alexandria, the kingdoms of the east, and of all the kingdoms of future ages — I alone will give you all these, if you kneel down and worship me' . . . 'Go away, Satan! The Scripture says, "Worship the Lord your God and serve only Him!"'

I have no fear now. The fading day brings peace and there is no terror of night.

Key 8: Wholeness

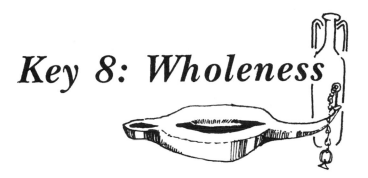

WHOLENESS

'Wholeness' and 'healing' are different terms to describe the same reality. However, 'healing' is often given a narrower, medical connotation, as if to suggest that there are two kinds of people in the world — sick people who need healing, and healthy people who do not. In reality, even those who are blessed with excellent physical health, may stand in great need of healing or wholeness in their emotional and spiritual selves. The exercises in this chapter deal with the deeper, more personal aspect of healing. That is the overcoming of the fear, anxiety, insecurity, anger, bitterness or bad habits that have trapped us, sometimes from our earliest childhood, and prevent us from living joyful, whole lives.

EXERCISE 32: RELAXATION AND HEALING MEDITATION

Lie flat on your back and relax. Take a little time to check on your breathing . . . heart-beat . . . awareness of the points of contact between your body and the floor. Before going on to this healing meditation, reflect on the ways in which you are in need of healing at this time. Are you physically unwell in any way? What hurts or painful memories have you been carrying? Think for a few moments of some one way in which you would particularly like God to give you healing during this time of meditation. Now resolve to leave the matter and your entire life completely in His hands. As you become more deeply relaxed, understand that you will be 'letting go' of your anxieties and concerns. In the words of Saint Peter: 'Leave all your worries with Him, because He cares for you' (I *Peter* 5.7).

Now become aware of your left hand . . . your left thumb. Visualise the thumb enlarged. Picture in your mind the surface of the skin with its folds and the nail. Imagine the tissue, blood vessels, muscles and nerves that lie beneath the skin. Going deeper, picture the bone structure, joints, marrow. While you are doing all this, sense all this detail within the thumb itself. As your awareness of your thumb is heightened, you will find that it becomes more and more relaxed. Move your attention up and down the thumb from the base, through the joints right up to the tip; and back down again. You may do this a number of times if you wish.

From the base of the thumb slowly move round into the base of the left index finger. Move slowly up along this finger through the three joints up to the finger-tip, maintaining as vivid an awareness of the inner structure as you can. Coming back down the index finger, slowly move round into the base of the middle finger. Move your attention up and down the middle finger, just as you did for the thumb and index finger. From there move on in turn through the ring finger and the little finger.

From the base of the little finger, move on to the palm of your left hand. Cover the whole surface of the palm and move slowly beneath the skin surface and right through to the back of the hand. From the back of the hand pass on to the wrist . . . through the wrist and on to the forearm. Bring your attention slowly up along the forearm . . . through the elbow . . . upper arm . . .

shoulder joint and shoulder-blade. The degree of relaxation that you will achieve in doing this will depend on how detailed you are able to visualise and sense each particular part of your body. So, as you practise this exercise at first, go through it as slowly as you can without losing concentration.

When you have brought your awareness as far as your left shoulder-blade, stop and have a general 'sense' of all of your left arm and hand, and how relaxed it is. Next, move slowly down the left side of your chest . . . left rib-cage . . . left side of abdomen . . . of pelvis and hip. Pass through the hip and in to your left thigh. Inch your way down the thigh . . . through the knee . . . calf . . . ankle . . . foot. From the foot move into the big toe. From there take in the second toe . . . third . . . fourth . . . and little toe. Then, on to the ball of the foot . . . sole . . . heel . . . back of heel . . . back of ankle . . . back of calf . . . back of knee . . . back of thigh . . . buttock . . . and left hip.

Pause now and generally become aware of your entire left leg and foot. Then take in together your left leg and left arm and the entire left side of your body. Bring your attention across to the right side of your body and briefly note the difference between the two sides — how much more relaxed and alive your left side feels. Quickly move on to your right hand. Focus on your right thumb. Go through the entire sequence described above, substituting 'right' for 'left'. Finish up with an awareness of your right leg, arm and side fully relaxed and alive. Then take in both right and left sides together — your whole body relaxed.

Bring your attention now to the centre of your body, to your navel. Become aware of, and relax in turn, the area around your navel . . . genital area . . . rectum . . . solar plexus . . . heart . . . throat. Move upwards to

your lower jaw . . . tongue . . . lower lip . . . upper lip
. . . left cheek . . . right cheek . . . both cheeks
together . . . left eye socket . . . right eye socket . . .
the entire area around your eyes . . . left eyebrow . . .
right eyebrow . . . forehead . . . scalp . . . top of head
. . . back of head . . . neck . . . and shoulders. Become
aware of and relax each part of your back, starting at the
neck and moving slowly down, vertebra by vertebra, until
you come to the base of the spine. You have now relaxed,
through awareness, all of the main parts of your body
individually.

You are now ready to move on to the healing
meditation proper. Picture in front of your mind the
figure of a square. Inside the square there is a circle, the
circle being slightly smaller than
the square and not touching it.
Inside the circle there is an equilateral triangle pointing upwards.
the triangle being smaller than
the circle and not touching.
Slowly move towards the figure,
observing it becoming larger as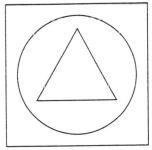
you approach it. Veer to the the left and continue
moving until you are just outside the left side of the
square. Look closely at the side of the square. What is it
made out of? . . . what colour? . . . what is it like to
touch? Pass slowly through the side of the square, so that
you are inside the square but outside the circle, and
pause there. The square is a symbol of God. It represents
his integrity, his truth, his faithfulness and his
dependability. Rest for a while 'within God', listening to
his healing words: 'I am the Lord, the one who heals
you' (*Exodus* 15.26).

Next turn your attention to the circle. Take note of its
colour and texture, and what it feels like. Slowly pass

through the side of the circle to the inside, but remain outside the triangle. The circle represents the fullness of God, his generosity, warmth and love. Listen awhile to his words: 'I will heal . . . and restore them to health. I will show them abundant peace and security' (*Jeremiah* 33.6).

Finally, take note of the triangle, its colour . . . material . . . what it feels like. Pass through the side as before, but this time moving right to the centre of the triangle and relax there, feeling yourself 'protected' by the triangle inside the circle inside the square. The triangle represents the trinity of God: Father, Son and Holy Spirit. Rest within God's protection, listening as he speaks to you in any or all of the following texts:

'Come to me, all of you who are tired from carrying heavy loads, and I will give you rest. Take my yoke and put it on you, and learn from me, because I am gentle and humble in spirit; and you will find rest' (*Matthew* 11.28-29).

'For you who obey me, my saving power will rise on you like the sun and bring healing like the sun's rays' (*Malachi* 4.2).

'I will make you well again; I will heal your wounds (*Jeremiah* 30.17).

'I tell you: when you pray and ask for something, believe that you have received it, and you will be given whatever you ask for. And when you stand and pray, forgive anything you may have against anyone, so that your Father in heaven will forgive the wrongs you have done' (*Mark* 11.24-25).

Take as much time as you like during this, the most important part of the meditation. It is at this time that you are likely to be touched by the power of Christ's healing love. We can never know beforehand what exactly God wants to do for us and within us. Nevertheless, the entire process of slowing down and relaxing deeply can help us greatly to let go of our subconscious rigidity and resistance to being healed. Moving towards the centre of the triangle in stages helps us focus in on the words of Scripture. All of this means that we become more receptive during the meditation to the healing that the Lord so much wants us to have.

You are not of course limited to the selection of texts given above. Feel completely free to browse through the Scriptures and make your own personal choice. Best are lines in which Jesus or (in the *Old Testament*) God is shown speaking of his saving power or love towards his people.

Conclude your meditation by coming away slowly from the centre of the triangle through the side into the circle, and from there to the square and finally outside the figure. Withdraw gradually and as you do, observe the figure becoming smaller . . . still smaller . . . and eventually disappearing.

Remind yourself that you have been involved in a healing meditation. Become aware of your body, especially any part that has been injured or diseased. Become aware of your self generally, as you lie there deeply relaxed. Thank God for any improvement in you that you find or that may indeed be taking place at this moment.

Begin slowly to move your hands and feet. Raise your arms above your head in a stretching movement. Bring them down again and roll over on your side. Remain in silence for a while.

> **HEALING MEDITATION SUMMED UP**
>
> 1. Relax
>
> 2. Become aware of your body
>
> (especially injured or sick parts)
>
> 3. Move into the square . . . circle
>
> . . . triangle
>
> 4. Listen to the healing Word of God

EXERCISE 33: COPING WITH RESENTMENT

The hurts that we have received at the hands of others may call for a specific kind of healing meditation. We may feel so embittered towards those whom we see as having caused us to suffer, that we are unable to forgive or be reconciled with them. As Christians we know that we are called to forgive and leave the past behind us. Yet somehow we cannot bring ourselves to be other than angry or resentful. And our very inability to forgive leaves us feeling guilty and depressed. This meditation is designed to help ease the pains we pick up in our human relationships and so be able to forgive brother/sister from our heart (see *Matthew* 18.35).

Settle yourself down comfortably and relax your body. Use your imagination to reconstruct any scene from the Passion of Our Lord (*cf.* exercises 14, 16 and 17 on techniques for sitting still and turning the senses inwards). You may select from the agony at Gethsemani, Jesus scourged and crowned with thorns, or carrying his cross, or being crucified and hanging on the cross. Some preliminary reading from one of the gospel accounts will help you here. The important thing is that you take sufficient time to slow down and get into the scene. Note the details of the place where Jesus is — indoor/outdoor, day/night. Is it warm or cold? What other people are there? Pick them out individually and look at them closely. What sounds can you hear, what words are being spoken? Note the accents and feelings going with the words. Be present in the situation. Where do you place yourself — separately watching from a distance . . . among the disciples . . . the Jews . . . the Roman soldiers . . . the Pharisees?

Focus in on Jesus. Look at him closely . . . the marks on his body . . . his distress, exhaustion and pain. Let yourself be drawn to his eyes as they meet your eyes. What are his feelings towards you at this moment as he suffers for you? To help you with your reflections at this stage you might like to draw on some lines from the Prophet *Isaiah* (chapters 52 and 53):

'Many people were shocked when they saw him; he was so disfigured that he hardly looked human' (52.14).

'We despised him and rejected him; he endured suffering and pain' (53.3).

'But he endured the suffering that should have been ours, the pain that we should have borne' (53.4).

'Because of our sins he was wounded, beaten because of the evil we did. We are healed by the punishment he suffered, made whole by the blows he received' (53.5).

'He took the place of many sinners and prayed that they might be forgiven' (53.12).

As you ponder the sufferings of Jesus and his love for you, become aware of your feelings towards him: love, gratitude, repentance. Let your mind rest and take a little time just to 'be with' him.

115

When your sense of being in the presence of a loving God is well established, you may gently and only for a few moments at first begin to think about some person or persons who in the past has wronged or hurt you. Then quickly return to your awareness of Jesus. You can repeat the process a number of times, allowing yourself to become progressively more aware of the person who has embittered you. It is very important that you do not let your consciousness of your pain become greater than your consciousness of the great love that Jesus has for you — hence the need to keep on returning to the Passion scene before negative feelings have a chance to develop.

When you have been doing this for some time, you may feel ready to bring those who have hurt you into the gospel picture. See them among the people there, their eyes also meeting with the eyes of Jesus. How does Jesus see them? What feelings does Jesus have towards them? Now once again face Jesus. What is he saying to you out of his pain and love? Remain in silence for some time.

As you bring this meditation to a close, note any change that has taken place in your attitude and feelings towards those whom you have resented and felt bitter about for so long. Usually people find that they feel less bitter even after doing the exercise just once. However, complete healing generally comes about only through repeated meditation over a period of time on the Lord's Passion.

Finish up by thanking God for whatever blessings you may have received during this meditation.

EXERCISE 34: DEATH AND RESURRECTION

The final act of healing or being made whole can only come about through the experience of death, which the

Christian faith sees not as an end to life, but rather as a stepping into a new and richer life — the life that Jesus has through his Resurrection. As Jesus himself puts it: 'A grain of wheat remains no more than a single grain unless it is dropped into the ground and dies. If it does die, then it produces many grains' (*John* 12.24). For us, too, death is simply a part of the cycle: Life-death-greater life. To the extent that we can accept this truth about death, we will come to know a deepening peace within us — even though dying means letting go of our body, our conscious mind, our loved ones and everything we have and own in this world.

Lie flat on your back. Become aware of your body sensations. Allow some time for your breathing and your heart-beat to slow down. When you are fully relaxed, close your eyes and focus on your sense of hearing, just noting the different sounds that are round about you. Next bring your attention back to the breath. Note its speed and its depth. Remind yourself that one day you will be lying there just like this, but dead. You will die just as surely as Jesus died. Yet, through faith you can also rise like him from the dead. Reflect for some moments on the words of Saint Paul: 'When we were baptised into union with Christ Jesus, we were baptised into union with his death. By our baptism, then, we were buried with him and shared his death, in order that, just as Christ was raised from death by the glorious power of the Father, so also we might live a new life' (*Romans* 6.3-4).

Bring your attention now to your out-breath. Each time you breathe out, imagine that your body is slowly sinking into the ground. With each exhalation allow yourself to descend into your 'grave'. During this time you might keep in mind the words 'we were buried with him and shared his death'. As you let go of each breath, inch your way downwards, until you are just beneath the ground; then one foot below . . . two feet . . . three . . . four . . . five . . . six feet below. Rest there for a little while. You might imagine that you are lying in the tomb of Jesus, like him surrendering your life to God.

As you lie there, you might reflect on words like: 'Let me end my days like one of God's people; let me die in peace like the righteous' (*Numbers* 23.10); 'Whoever believes in me will live, even though he dies' (*John* 11.25).

Next move your attention away from your exhalation to your inhalation. As you draw in your breath, bring to mind the words 'as Christ was raised from death by the glorious power of the Father, we too might live a new life'. Each time you inhale begin to come up inch by inch from the bottom of the 'grave'. As you breathe in,  accept with gratitude and love the 'new life' that God is offering you. As you near the surface of the ground, become more and more aware that you are being called to share in the life of Jesus' resurrection and a peace and happiness that is beyond human understanding. At the end of your upward movement, remain still and silent on the floor for some time, if you wish, meditating on the words: 'dying, you destroyed our death; rising, your re-stored our life'; 'he who believes has eternal life' (*John*

6.47) or 'whoever hears my words and believes in him who sent me has eternal life' (*John* 5.24).

You may find yourself a bit reluctant to do this particular meditation. Death is a subject that most of us would rather not be reminded of. Still less may we want to visualise and meditate on our own death and burial. And yet, it is in facing the mystery of death that we will overcome our fears. A mature acceptance of the truth about my personal death and resurrection in Christ can give me a sense of joy and a freedom to live my life fully each day as it is given to me to live it. Such an acceptance is possible because a loving God is there to give me in return a far superior life to the one I am leaving behind.

The first time you approach this exercise, you may like to simply lie in the corpse posture (see exercise 10) for a few minutes, or go through the different stages of the meditation quickly. Later on, as you feel ready for it, you can enter into it more deeply. The more difficult part of the exercise is the first stage, where the emphasis is on letting go, dying, going down. Be gentle with yourself as you go through this part. Always give at least as much time and attention to the second ('rising') stage, for the truth is that death is overcome by resurrection (see I *Corinthians* 15.54-56).

Meditating on death/resurrection in a Christian context will help you cope with the fear of dying. You will come to understand more fully that there is so much more to your life than the life of your body. Such meditation is very different from a morbid fascination with death — the kind that can freeze your will to act and paralyse your capacity for worthwhile human and social involvement. On the contrary, to the extent that you have rightly come to terms with death, you will be happier and freer to love. You will have become a more whole person.

119

The perfect example of the 'whole man' (for Christians) is Jesus. Becoming whole involves sharing in the death and resurrection of Jesus, but also from day to day trying to live the kind of life that Jesus lived, both in his attitude to his heavenly Father and to people. Meditation can greatly help us grow in this kind of wholeness. The final exercise is designed to help us focus our minds and hearts on the person of Jesus, to open us up to the call that he makes on each one of us to follow him, to model ourselves on him.

EXERCISE 35: FOLLOWING JESUS

This is a meditation on the Call of the Disciples in the gospel of *Matthew* 4.18-22 (and corresponding passages in other gospels). First, prepare yourself for this meditation by slowly reading the whole passage through and then, sitting comfortably (*cf.* exercise 14). Move into your 'inner space' as explained in exercise 16. Next turn your five senses of seeing, hearing, taste, touch and smell inwards and focus them on the gospel scene. The following notes can be used to help you 'witness' Jesus calling the first four of his disciples.

A beautiful still lake, surrounded by a range of low hills — daytime, sun sparkling on water — boats drawn up along a gravelly shore, primitive wooden constructions with makeshift oars and sails — old worn nets spread out to dry.

Fishermen with bearded bronzed complexions, clad in cheap tattered clothing — Galilee is a poor backward area, even by the standards of the time. There are many fishermen, including two brothers, Simon and Andrew. They are among a group that are attempting to catch fish by casting nets from the shore. Others are repairing the damage done to their nets from getting caught on the edges of rocks or perhaps (all too rarely) from getting an exceptionally heavy catch. Among these we find old Zebedee and his two sons, James and John.

A common everyday scene, not the kind of situation likely to produce anything out of the ordinary — 'Nothing ever happens round here!' you can almost hear one of the younger men saying, 'Nothing to do except work on the lake all day — and half the night as well'.

An unfamiliar figure appears on the scene, calmly walking along the shore — a stranger, certainly not a man of the lake — no fisherman's walk that! 'What's he doing around here?' The stranger stops near the group who are fishing, fixes his gaze on Simon, half-smiling to himself, but says nothing. One by one all the fishermen stop their conversation and their work and turn to stare at the stranger. What an extraordinary person he is — seems almost to be able to see into your soul!

And now he speaks: 'Come with me, and I will teach you to catch men' — and turns and moves off. And what's this? 'Simon! Andrew! Where are you off to? What about the nets?'

The curious trio proceeds downshore to Zebedee's boat. The stranger once again creates the same irresistible fascination on all whom he meets. This time it is Zebedee's two sons, James and John. They follow the stranger without as much as a parting word to their father. The likes of it was never seen on the lake before — or since.

Having visualised the action of the gospel scene, now centre your attention on Jesus alone. At the same time, get in touch with your breathing. Keeping the image of Jesus as you imagine him before your mind, recite mentally the following litany to the rhythm of your breathing, one phrase each time you breathe out:

Jesus, the stranger	Jesus, risen from the dead
Jesus, son of God	Jesus, at the right hand of God
Jesus, son of Mary and Joseph	Jesus, my Lord
Jesus, existing from eternity	Jesus, my judge
Jesus, born into time	Jesus my friend
Jesus, creator of the universe	Jesus, who forgives me
Jesus, a helpless baby	Jesus, who saves me
Jesus, growing up in Nazareth	Jesus, who heals me
Jesus, preaching the good news	Jesus, in the Scriptures
Jesus, healing the sick	Jesus, in the Eucharist
Jesus, raising the dead	Jesus, in the Church
Jesus, eating with sinners	Jesus, in people
Jesus, at the Last Supper	Jesus, in those who suffer
Jesus, in Gethsemani	Jesus, in me
Jesus, scourged and crowned with thorns	Jesus, loving me now
Jesus, crucified	Jesus, speaking to me now
Jesus, dead and buried	Jesus, calling me now

'COME, FOLLOW ME . . .'

The regular silent repetition of the name Jesus will help you to keep your mind stilled on the Lord. Mentally 'whispering' different aspects of the life of Jesus will make it easier for you to remain alert and not become distracted. You do not, of course, have to use the list of attributes or associated ideas given — feel free to compose your own. You need not have more than half a dozen if you prefer. The list that will work best in your meditation, that will help you become absorbed, mind and heart, in the Lord, will be the list of qualities that mean most to you personally. You may, for instance, decide to select just a few lines and repeat them several times. Whichever way you decide to use the litany technique, remain in silence for at least a few minutes after you finish.

IF YOU WANT TO KNOW MORE...

These pages summarise experience gained over a period of eighteen years. During the first six years of that period, I lectured in philosophy and theology at St Charles' Seminary, Nagpur in India. As I taught, I also began learning what I could about India, her culture and religion, and especially yoga. I practised yogic postures and breathing, studied and experimented with techniques of concentration, sifting out those that I found could help my own Christian meditation. On returning to Ireland I began to share my experience of blending yoga skills with Christian spirituality. For a number of years I have been giving seminars and retreats in many places, but most of all in my home base, St Dominic's Priory and Retreat Centre, Ennismore, Montenotte, Cork. The exercises in this book have long been tried and tested firstly by myself and then by many of the people who have come to us on retreats.

The treatment of yoga postures given in chapter 3 (exercise 10) is highly condensed because of limited space. You can learn much more by going to a competent yoga teacher. Not all are equally good. Those that are affiliated to recognised yoga fellowships or have been trained in India are generally reliable from a technical point of view. However, you may have to check the motives of some of them. They just may be teaching you in order to convert you to their brand of Hinduism. If that is what you are looking for, then that's fine.

What are the long-term effects of meditation?

After working for some weeks at one or more of the exercises in this book, you may well begin to feel as if you have been peeling an onion. You may (possibly for the first time) have been made aware of just how restless the mind is. After an initial period during which you found meditation both physically and mentally relaxing, you may now not be finding much satisfaction in the practice. You will be tempted to abandon it altogether. Resist the temptation!

The fact that your meditation is not now proving as emotionally and physically satisfying as it did earlier on, is a sign that you are beginning to make progress. As you are being drawn to a deeper stillness within your body and within your self, your conscious mind and your emotions are not taking too kindly to the fact that they are no longer the centre of attention when you sit down to meditate. You will feel a certain 'boredom' at the level of your thoughts. If you can persevere nonetheless, you will begin to discover in the deepest part of your being, a new and unshakeable peace, a deep harmony and a 'rightness'. You will have come a little closer to God or perhaps, recognised a little more clearly that he was, and is, there all the time.

Is there really such a thing as Christian meditation?

You will know that your meditation is especially Christian from the fact that instead of being an unbroken series of 'high's, it calls you to suffer as well as to be at peace. The suffering takes a number of different forms — the discipline of giving up whatever you are doing and (unless immediate duty dictates otherwise) sitting down regularly for a fixed period of time; endless re-focusing of your attention every time it wanders during meditation; facing down your fear of being there without moving, not thinking, not sensing — but simply experiencing inner silence and aloneness. Yet that pain, if we accept it, leads us on to glory, for we are accepting an emptiness that allows the risen Lord to enter deep within us. Christian meditation means dying and rising with Jesus, all within the space of half-an-hour, each time you meditate.

How often and for how long should I meditate?

A general norm of twenty to thirty minutes twice a day should be aimed at, but this should be adapted where necessary. Those with heavy family or work responsibilities, parents of young children, those who are sick and young people might have to be satisfied with one ten to fifteen minute period of meditation daily. In the very beginning you might stay at it for as little as five to ten minutes, then building up gradually towards your norm.

At the other end of the scale, two hour-long meditations daily should be regarded as the maximum regular daily practice, unless you are an experienced meditator or are practising under a qualified spiritual guide. Such prolonged meditation, especially on the part of a beginner, runs the risk of leading to hallucinations, impairment of the ability to relate to other people and a general inability to cope with the practical demands of life.

Having decided on the arrangement most suited to you, it is important thereafter that you stick to it. Begin

and end your meditation at a fixed time each morning/
evening, irrespective of how you may be feeling.
Remember, in meditation you are living your life at a
level that is much deeper than your feelings or emotions.

*What about hallucinations, visions, stranges sounds and
psychic phenomena?*

Strange sensations, inner lights and sounds, feelings
— both sweet and unpleasant — can occasionally occur
during meditation. Do not take too much notice of them
— they may simply be your senses and emotions craving
attention. Just continue with your meditation — focusing
on the Lord, 'hearing' your mantra, keeping your
awareness where it should be. For the most part, these
'spectacular effects' are of no great significance and in
time will fade away by themselves.

If however, you experience repeatedly any frightening
'presences', then this might be a problem that needs to
be dealt with specifically. The best thing is to seek
competent spiritual advice, before continuing with that
particular method of meditating. Such phenomena may
be the residue of earlier negative spiritual experiences,
particularly those involving ouija boards, seances or
other psychic activities. They can also come about as a
result of drug abuse or membership of bizarre religious
cults. They may need to be remedied by some special
from of spiritual healing.

Can meditation be selfish or escapist?

It is difficult to know exactly one's own motivation
when one meditates. There are however, a few indi-
cations that you should look out for as you go along. Ask
yourself: am I neglecting any responsibilities to my family

and others as a result of the time and attention I give to meditation? Do I see my meditation merely as a cosy refuge from the challenges of life, a way of (literally) closing my eyes to what God is really asking of me? Am I constantly looking out for 'beautiful experiences' from my meditation? Do I meditate primarily in order to develop my mental powers? Is meditation making me more self-centred and less concerned with the well-being of others? If the answer to any of these questions is 'yes', then your meditation is to some extent self-indulgent.

Meditation should be undertaken without any particular expectation of what is 'supposed to happen'. It is not about getting something for yourself, but about giving yourself to God. Of course, as you become over time a more tranquil and spiritual person, you will know a greater joy than you have ever had in your life — but don't look for it, just let it happen when and if it happens. Seek God and his plan for you and your meditation will be anything but escapist. You will become a less self-centred and more loving person. 'Be concerned above everything else with the Kingdom of God and with what he requires of you, and he will provide you with all these other things' (*Matthew* 6.33).